100 NOTTINGHAMSHIRE
GREATS County Cricket Club

George Gunn is flanked by his two sons, Jack and George Vernon, in a trial match at Trent Bridge in his final season.

100 GREATS

NOTTINGHAMSHIRE
COUNTY CRICKET CLUB

COMPILED BY
JIM LEDBETTER

TEMPUS

KEY

Batting and bowling styles for each player are designated by the following letters:

RHB – right-handed batsman
LHB – left handed batsman
RF – right-arm fast
LF – left-arm fast
RFM – right-arm fast medium
LM – left-arm medium pace
RM – right-arm medium pace
OB – off-break bowler
SLA – slow left-arm spin
LB – leg-break
RS – right-arm slow
WK – wicketkeeper

First published 2003

Tempus Publishing Limited
The Mill, Brimscombe Port,
Stroud, Gloucestershire, GL5 2QG

British Library Cataloguing in Publication Data.
A catalogue record for this book is available from the British Library.

ISBN 0 7524 2745 8

Typesetting and origination by Tempus Publishing Limited
Printed in Great Britain by Midway Colour Print, Wiltshire

Acknowledgements

I would like to thank Derek Drake for supplying me with the career records of both the county's earliest players and the current playing staff, and for listening over a lengthy period to my observations on which cricketers to select or omit from the final one hundred names. This book would have taken much longer and proved much more difficult to write had it not been for the invaluable assistance of friend and ACS colleague Peter Wynne-Thomas. His own writings on Nottinghamshire cricket alone provided a treasure trove of information, but he was also kind enough to allow me to consult his own files on the cricketers listed in this book. Many enlightening conversations took place in the Trent Bridge Library. He was kind enough to read through the initial manuscript, alerting me to a number of errors and misjudgements. I would also like to thank him for the use of photographs and illustrations of the players which are housed in the Trent Bridge Library. In particular, I am grateful for a number of photographs of individual players from the collection of Duncan Anderson, which was donated to the Trent Bridge Library. Many thanks also to James Howarth of Tempus Publishing for giving me the opportunity to write this book and thanks to Ruth Potter, Kate Wiseman and Becky Gadd for their helpfulness in putting it together. At a time when many publishers are loath to support specialist cricket books, it is refreshing to find one which is so supportive in this field. Finally, my thanks to Sam Bowles of Bowles Associates for supplying the cover photograph of Paul Johnson.

Preface

Since Nottinghamshire's inaugural match in 1826, when the county met a combined Sheffield and Leicester XI at Sheffield, 575 individuals have played for the county in three-day and limited-overs matches. Out of these, I have selected one hundred whom I consider have made the greatest contribution to the fortunes of the county in its 176-year history up to the close of the 2002 season. The only players excluded from consideration were those whose appearances were limited to two seasons or less.

The final list of one hundred Nottinghamshire cricketers has resulted in some interesting findings. The most gratifying conclusion was that seventy-four players were qualified to play for Nottinghamshire by reasons of either birth or residence. It is all the more heartening as the county, forced by increasingly poor results, abandoned in 1950 its long-held cherished principle of selecting only Nottinghamshire players. Recruitment from other counties and overseas followed, bringing fleeting success with the signing of world-class players such as Bruce Dooland and Gary Sobers. However, it was the combination of overseas players, Clive Rice and Richard Hadlee, assisted by a new generation of local talent, in particular Derek Randall, Bruce French and Tim Robinson, which finally brought about a decade of achievement in the 1980s. The current side represents a cosmopolitan mix of Australians, South Africans, county imports and more than a fair sprinkling of local players. The most encouraging recent development has been the emergence of local Asian players, who have learnt their cricket in this county. Usman Afzaal has already played for England whilst Bilal Shafayat, the present England Under-19 captain, is one of the most exciting prospects seen at Trent Bridge since the war.

The numbers of players appearing for the county in different eras represents the varying fortunes of the Nottinghamshire eleven. Twenty-six played most of their cricket prior to 1900, reflecting the strength of Nottinghamshire cricket in the nineteenth century. It had been Nottinghamshire men, such as William Clarke, George Parr and Richard Daft, who had played vital roles in the spread of cricket throughout England and abroad. Other outstanding cricketers were Alfred Shaw, who bowled the first ball in Test cricket, Arthur Shrewsbury, the first to reach 1,000 Test runs, and William Gunn, the first of a great Nottinghamshire cricketing dynasty, later to be followed by John, one of the county's most successful all-rounders, and George, one of its greatest characters. In comparison, only forty-one have played all their first-class cricket after 1945 – a sign of the county's fall from grace over many decades since the Second World War.

The types of players included in the one hundred can be approximately classified as forty-five batsmen, thirty-five bowlers, twelve all-rounders and eight wicketkeepers. Amongst the batsmen are a relatively high proportion of openers, many of whom were to open for England. The county has been fortunate to have possessed many highly successful opening pairs, A.O. Jones and Jimmy Iremonger, George Gunn and 'Dodge' Whysall, Wally Keeton and Charlie Harris and, most recently, Tim Robinson and Chris Broad.

If the county has continued to produce high-quality batsmen throughout its history, Joe Hardstaff Jnr, Reg Simpson, Derek Randall and Tim Robinson all being examples of post-war players who have proved successful at the highest level, the same cannot be said of its bowlers. The county was renowned for its great attack in the nineteenth century, bowlers of pre-Test days such as Clarke, Tinley, Grundy, Wootton and Jackson, being followed by five bowlers who were selected for England before the turn of the century. The Championship of 1907 was won largely through the match-winning performances of Hallam and Wass, the latter being one of the greatest bowlers never to have been selected for England. Larwood and Voce maintained this tradition in the interwar years, but since 1946, the only Nottinghamshire-born bowler to make his debut for England has been Harold Butler.

Most of the county's leading run-scorers and wicket-takers find a place in this book. Only two batsmen who have scored over 7,000 runs for the county, Ron Giles and Paul Todd, are missing. Amongst the bowlers, Kevin Evans with 364 wickets is the only bowler with over 350 wickets not to be included. All three were among the final ten or so peripheral players who were considered for the top one hundred. Of the eligible players, five double-centurions failed to make the cut, as did one bowler who has taken nine wickets in an innings and two takers of a hat-trick. Answers on a postcard please!

The county has also benefited from some excellent overseas signings since the war. If one includes Carlton Forbes, Gamini Goonesena and Basharat Hassan in this category, eight are to be found in this publication, with Deryck Murray, the West Indian wicketkeeper being unfortunate not to be included.

As well as the inclusion of the forty players who played for their country whilst appearing for the county and the twenty-five who have been named as one of *Wisden*'s Cricketers of the Year, a number surpassed by only four other counties, there is also room for many cricketers who gave of their best when the county was enduring hard times, especially so in the post-war decades. Arthur Jepson, Barry Stead and Norman Hill are just three examples from a number of players who fall into this category.

I wish to dedicate this book to fellow-members of the Trent Bridge Taverners, knowledgeable lovers of the game and consistently loyal supporters of Nottinghamshire teams through both good times and bad. Watching cricket at Trent Bridge is a great pleasure in itself, but almost equally satisfying is cricket conversation. I hope this book may contribute an additional ingredient to the forthcoming season's talk in the Larwood and Voce Stand.

Bibliography

The sources consulted are too numerous to list in full. In addition to the following periodicals, *Wisden Cricketer's Almanack* 1864-2002, *Cricket* 1882-1913, *The Cricketer* 1921 to date, *Playfair Cricket Monthly* 1960-1973, the *Playfair Cricket Annual* 1948 to date, *Wisden Cricket Monthly* 1979 to date, *Cricket Lore* 1991 to date, the *Cricketer's Who's Who* 1981 to date, and various local newspapers, the following publications have been of particular value.

Reference
A. Haygarth, *Scores and Biographies*
P. Bailey, P. Thorn and P. Wynne-Thomas, *Who's Who of Cricketers*
R. Brooke, *A History of the County Championship*
—, *Cricket Milestones*

W. Frindall, *The Wisden Book of Cricket Records*
W. Frindall, *England Test Cricketers*
J. Ledbetter, *First-Class Cricket, A Complete Record 1930-39*
Notts CCC, Yearbooks 1947 to date
J.F. Sutton, *Nottingham Cricket Matches 1771-1865*
C.H. Richards, *Nottinghamshire Cricket Scores and Biographies 1865-77*
P. Wynne-Thomas, *Nottinghamshire Cricketers 1821-1914*
—, *Nottinghamshire Cricketers 1919-1939*
—, *Nottinghamshire CCC First-Class Records 1826-1995*

Other Publications
J. Arlott, *'Rough Diamond' (Tom Wass) Arlott on Cricket*
—, *Alletson's Innings*
F.S. Ashley-Cooper, *Nottinghamshire Cricket and Cricketers*
G. Broadribb, *The Lost Art. A History of Under-arm Bowling*
D. Carew, *England Over*
—, *To The Wicket*
N. Cardus, *Days in the Sun, The Summer Game, Cricket, Second Innings, Close of Play*
A.W. Carr, *Cricket With The Lid Off*
S. Chalke, *Runs in the Memory*
—, *Caught in the Memory*
—, *One More Run*
R. Daft, *Kings of Cricket*
D. Frith, *Bodyline Autopsy*
R. Hadlee, *Rhythm and Swing*
B. Haynes & J. Lucas, *The Trent Bridge Battery; The Story of the Sporting Gunns.*
H. Larwood, *Bodyline?*
E.V. Lucas, *A Hundred Years of Trent Bridge*
M. Marshall, *Gentlemen and Players*
A.W. Pullin, *Alfred Shaw – Cricketer*
R.C. Robertson-Glasgow, *Cricket Prints. Some Batsmen and Bowlers 1920-1940*
—, *More Cricket Prints. Some Batsmen and Bowlers 1920-1945*
R. Sissons, *The Players*
D.G. West, *The Elevens of England*
P. Wynne-Thomas, *Give Me Arthur*
—, *Trent Bridge*
—, *Nottinghamshire;Cricket's Double Champions 1987*
—, *Rags*

Publications of the Association of Cricket Statisticians and Historians
Statistical Surveys, 1863-1878
ACS Yearbooks, 1986-2002
First-Class Match Scores, 1801-1905
P.E. Dyson, *Benson & Hedges Cup Record Book 1972-1994*
H. Garrod, *A.O.Jones*
L. Hatton, *Sunday League Record Book 1969-1992*
G. Hudd, *Reg Simpson*
V. and R. Isaacs, *NatWest Trophy Record Book 1963-96*
K.A.P. Sandiford, *Gary Sobers*
P. Wynne-Thomas, *Harold Larwood*
—, *George Parr*

100 Nottinghamshire Greats

Andy Afford
Usman Afzaal
Ted Alletson
Dick Attewell
Billy Barnes
Fred Barratt
Darren Bicknell
Sam Biddulph
Thomas Bignall
John Birch
Brian Bolus
Chris Broad
Harold Butler
Chris Cairns
Arthur Carr
William Clarke
John Clay
Kevin Cooper
John Cotton
Richard Daft
Ian Davison
John Dixon
Bruce Dooland
Wilfred Flowers
Carlton Forbes
Paul Franks
Bruce French
Jason Gallian
Gamini Goonesena
James Grundy
George Gunn
George Vernon Gunn
John Gunn
William Gunn

Joseph Guy
Richard Hadlee
Albert Hallam
Joe Hardstaff, (Snr)
Joe Hardstaff, (Jnr)
Charlie Harris
Mike Harris
'Basher' Hassan
George Heane
Eddie Hemmings
Maurice Hill
Norman Hill
Jimmy Iremonger
John Jackson
Arthur Jepson
Paul Johnson
A.O. Jones
Wally Keeton
Harold Larwood
Chris Lewis
Ben Lilley
Martin McIntyre
Frank Matthews
Eric Meads
Geoff Millman
Fred Morley
Thomas Oates
William Oscroft
George Parr
Wilfred Payton
Andy Pick
Paul Pollard
Cyril Poole
Derek Randall

Chris Read
Clive Rice
Len Richmond
Tim Robinson
William Scotton
John Selby
Frank Shacklock
Alfred Shaw
Jemmy Shaw
Mordecai Sherwin
Arthur Shrewsbury
Reg Simpson
Ken Smales
Mike Smedley
Gary Sobers
Arthur Staples
Sam Staples
Barry Stead
Franklyn Stephenson
Freddie Stocks
Mike Taylor
Chris Tinley
Bill Voce
Willis Walker
'Topsy' Wass
'Bomber' Wells
Bob White
'Dodge' Whysall
Frank Woodhead
George Wootton
Charles Wright
Frederick Wyld

The top twenty, who appear here in italics, occupy two pages instead of the usual one.

John Andrew Afford
RHB & SLA, 1984-97

Born: 15 May 1964, Crowland, Lincolnshire

Batting

M	I	NO	Runs	HS
168	166	71	398	22*
50	11	8	6	2*
Ave	50	100	ct/st	
4.18	-	-	56	
2.00	-	-	10	

Bowling

Runs	Wkts	Ave	BB	5wl	10wM
15302	464	32.97	6-51	16	2
1737	46	37.76	4-38	-	

Best Performances
22* v. Leicestershire, Nottingham, 1989
2 v. Buckinghamshire, Marlow, 1990*
6-51 v. Lancashire, Nottingham, 1996
4-38 v. Kent, Nottingham, 1989

An impressive record as a slow left-arm bowler in Lincolnshire junior representative sides in the early 1980s earned Afford a trial in 1984. Even before being offered a permanent place on the staff, he had made his first XI debut, appearing against Oxford University in the opening fixture of the season. A Championship debut followed, but it was not until 1986, after consistent wicket-taking in the Second XI, that he obtained a place in the county team, when he ousted Peter Such as the second spinner to Hemmings in the closing stages of the season.

With Notts in contention for the title, he contributed to their challenge with career-best innings and match figures against Kent, 6-81 and 10-103 respectively, nine wickets against Glamorgan in a close 24-run victory, whilst his eight wickets in the match against Northamptonshire almost secured another victory. Back injuries severely limited his appearances in the following two seasons, but he was to make one significant contribution to the Championship success of 1987. His nine wickets in the match against Championship leaders Yorkshire helped secure an eight-wicket victory, which after the county's indifferent start to the season, began a ten-match unbeaten run.

Between 1989 and 1993, he remained a permanent member of the side, taking over fifty wickets on four occasions, his performances in 1989 earning him a place in the England A tour to Zimbabwe, where he played in two one-day internationals and two unofficial Tests. With the departure of Hemmings, he effectively became the senior spinner in the side, taking most wickets and bowling most overs, but his position was soon challenged by the emergence of two young players, Afzaal and Hindson, both left-arm spinners. Hindson's loss of form and Afzaal's growing preoccupation with batting gave Afford the opportunity to play in every Championship fixture in 1996, heading the bowling averages and taking most wickets in what was his only season as an ever-present in the side.

Surprisingly, he was completely overlooked in 1997, being released at the end of the season. At best an indifferent fielder and a mediocre batsman, he was also unable to command a regular place in limited-overs cricket, although he was to play a memorable role in the county's success in the 1989 Benson & Hedges competition. In the semi-final against Kent, his four wickets in twenty-two balls halted Kent's hopes of passing the Notts total, and in the final against Essex, he claimed the important wicket of Graham Gooch at a time when he was well set. In all, Afford took 464 wickets for the county, putting him at 27th in the list of the county's wicket-takers. He is still involved in the game, both coaching and working in media projects for the Professional Cricketer's Association.

Usman Afzaal
LHB & SLA, 1995-

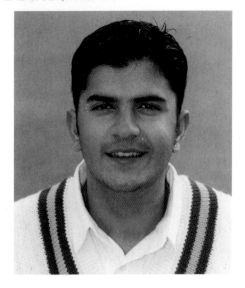

Born: 9 September 1977, Rawalpindi, Pakistan

Batting

M	I	NO	Runs	HS
110	192	16	5784	151*
81	71	14	2086	95*

Ave	50	100	ct/st	
32.86	34	11	55	
36.59	17	-	20	

Bowling

Runs	Wkts	Av	BB	5wI	10wM
3116	57	54.66	4-101	-	-
841	31	27.12	3-8	-	

Best Performances
151* Worcestershire, Nottingham, 2000
95 v. Hampshire, Southampton, 2000*
4-101 v. Gloucestershire, Nottingham, 1998
3-8 v. Ireland, Clontarf, 2002

Even before he began his first-class career, Usman Afzaal had given every indication of becoming a highly successful cricketer. He represented England at Under-15 and Under-17 levels and by 1993 he was appearing for the Nottinghamshire Second XI, initially as a left-arm spin-bowler. Although taking most wickets in 1995, he was also making his mark as a promising batsman, scoring just over 500 runs in the same season. His first-class debut against Kent in 1995, only thirteen days after his eighteenth birthday, must have been a chastening experience. The match produced an aggregate of 1,642 runs, the third largest aggregate in Championship history, with Afzaal's match figures being 0-164.

His development as a batsman, rather than a left-arm spin bowler, was confirmed by an excellent season in the Second XI in 1996, when he averaged 60.66 but achieved little with the ball. Two innings early in the 1997 season laid the basis of a regular place in the side. Called up for the third Championship fixture of the season, against Lancashire at Old Trafford, he proved his worth with two fighting innings on a lively pitch when early wickets had fallen cheaply, recording two unbeaten seventies and sharing two century partnerships with Paul Johnson.

Since then he has been an established member of the side, scoring his maiden hundred in the opening fixture of 1998, this being balanced by eight noughts, possibly a consequence of batting too high in the order at this stage of his career. However the county's belief in his ability paid off in 2000 when he passed 1,000 runs for the first time – a target he has reached in every subsequent season. However, it was his gritty, determined innings against Worcestershire, which attracted most attention. When Harris, the last man, joined him, Notts required 92 runs to avoid the follow-on with the Australian pace bowler McGrath in full cry. The pair added 152 for the last wicket, equalling the county record with Afzaal recording a career-best unbeaten 151*.

International recognition has since followed with tours to the West Indies with England A in 2000/01 and with the full England side to India and New Zealand in 2001/02. The highlight of his career so far has been his three Tests against Australia in 2000 when he scored an aggressive fifty, also taking the wicket of Adam Gilchrist with his third ball in Test cricket.

Although tried as an opening batsman and a number three, he appears to have found his real niche as a middle-order batsman, who has gradually increased his range of strokes and adopted a more positive approach to batting, reflected in his brilliant 134 against Essex in the final fixture of the 2002 season. Both confident and ambitious, he has now sufficient experience to again put himself into contention for an England place.

Edwin Boaler Alletson

RHB & RMLB, 1906-14

Born: 6 March 1884, Welbeck Woodhouse,
Nottinghamshire
Died: 5 July 1963, Worksop, Nottinghamshire

Batting

M	I	NO	Runs	HS
118	177	6	3194	189
Ave	50	100	ct/st	
18.67	13	1	73	

Bowling

Runs	Wkts	Av	BB	5wl	10wM
628	33	19.03	6-74	1	-

Best Performances
189 v. Sussex, Hove, 1911
6-74 v. Northamptonshire, Northampton, 1910

Alletson's Innings by John Arlott is one of the few cricket books devoted to one individual innings. A twenty-seven-year-old Nottinghamshire batsman, Ted Alletson, standing over 6ft and weighing 15st, played that innings against Sussex at Hove on the 20 May 1911. It was an unparalleled innings of sustained and ferocious hitting in the first-class game, which was to bring him his sole first-class hundred. It was his hitting against the bowling of Albert Hallam, renowned for his accuracy, during a game against the Notts Club and Ground which earned him a position on the Notts ground staff and eventually to a county debut in 1906. Although a regular member of the 1907 Championship-winning side, he achieved little of note, although it was noted in *Wisden* that 'it would not be easy to name a harder driver' and that he has 'such extraordinary hitting powers that he may at any time take a step to the front'. That prediction was to materialise at Hove in the county's second Championship fixture of the 1911 season.

Alletson was somewhat fortunate to play in this fixture, having sustained an injured wrist. When he came in to bat on the third morning in front of a small crowd, Nottinghamshire was facing an innings defeat, being only nine runs ahead with three wickets remaining. By lunch he had batted for fifty minutes for 47 runs but two further wickets had fallen, leaving Notts 84 ahead with one wicket to fall. Told during the

interval to have a go, in the next forty minutes he was to hit 142 out of the 152 runs put on for the last wicket, a county record, before being caught on the boundary. Five balls were lost, one being embedded in a timber post in the pavilion. A record 34 runs were struck off an over from Killick, which included two no-balls (4-6-6-4-4-4-6). His innings contained 8 sixes and 23 fours and took just ninety minutes. Alletson had simply stood in his crease and driven almost everything, deliberately getting right under the ball to lift it over the boundary, anywhere between long-on and deep extra-cover.

In the following game, Alletson hit 60 out of 80 in thirty minutes against Gloucestershire at Bristol and was subsequently chosen for the Test trial at Sheffield, the only non-Nottinghamshire fixture of Alletson's first-class career. He also received a gold watch from the Duke of Portland and a £100 cheque. He continued to play for the county until May 1914, although never again commanding a regular place. Alletson was a modest county batsman, but a great hitter who was capable of fast scoring on his day. His 13 fifties for the county were all rapid affairs and he also once hit three consecutive deliveries of Wilfred Rhodes for six in 1913. He carved himself a niche in cricket history with his one great innings. As Robert Relf, one of the Sussex fieldsmen, remarked, 'I don't think any man could have played two innings like that and lived.'

Born: 12 June 1861, Keyworth, Nottinghamshire
Died: 11 June 1927, Long Eaton, Derbyshire

Batting

M	I	NO	Runs	HS
283	419	37	5763	102
Ave	50	100	ct/st	
15.08	23	1	230	

Bowling

Runs	Wkts	Av	BB	5wI	10wM
20226	1303	15.52	9-23	95	19

Best Performances
102 v. Kent, Gravesend, 1897
9-23 v. Sussex, Nottingham, 1886

Dick Attewell, in terms of wickets taken, was the most successful of the many outstanding nineteenth-century Nottinghamshire bowlers. When his county career ended in 1900, he had claimed 1,303 wickets, a number surpassed subsequently by only two others. He was to capture eight wickets in an innings on seven occasions, his 9-23 against Sussex in 1886 being the county record at that time.

He dominated the Nottinghamshire bowling figures in his time, heading the county averages on thirteen occasions and in two other seasons capturing the most wickets. He was the second bowler after Morley to take 100 wickets in a season for the county, achieving this on four occasions, a record until later overtaken by Wass. Altogether he claimed 100 wickets in a season on ten occasions, heading the national averages in 1889 with 149 wickets at 10.97 apiece. His devotion to practice contributed to his exceptional accuracy, which allied to his easy graceful action, made him one of the most economical bowlers of all times. A right-arm medium-pace bowler with a round-arm action, he was capable of bowling long spells if necessary, but on a helpful pitch, his ability to make the ball nip from the off caused batsmen great difficulties. His economical bowling became legendary. His most economical four-ball over analysis was 46 runs off 89 overs against Kent in 1888 and five-ball, also against Kent, was 7 runs conceded in 25 overs.

His opportunity came in 1881 when seven of the leading professionals refused terms and were omitted from the team. He finished his first season with 35 wickets, the most by any Notts bowler, claiming career-best match figures of 13-134 against Sussex. Although the return of the old hands limited his chances in 1882, the illness and subsequent death of Frederick Morley opened the way for his automatic selection for the next seventeen seasons. His 100 wickets in all matches in 1884 helped Nottinghamshire to win nine out of their ten county fixtures and claim the title of Champion County. In the same year, his impressive performances against the Australians were followed by tours to Australia in 1884/85, 1887/88 and 1891/92, where he topped the bowling averages on the last two visits. His reputation as a bowler of economy was carried into the Test arena, Attewell conceding only 21.96 runs per 100 balls bowled.

He was also a very competent lower order batsman, scoring his only century towards the close of his career, saving the game against Kent with 102 at Gravesend in 1897. Aged 36 years and 7 days, he was the oldest Nottinghamshire player to score a maiden century until Keith Miller in 1959. On retirement, he became a first-class umpire from 1902-1907, standing in 130 first-class matches. As to his cricketing ability, it was stated in *Cricket* that 'It is seldom safe to say that such-and-such a man was the very best bowler of his day, but when Attewell was in his prime, it might truly have been said of him that he had no superiors.'

William Barnes

RHB & RFM, 1875-94

Born: 27 May 1852, Sutton-in-Ashfield, Nottinghamshire
Died: 24 March 1899, Mansfield Woodhouse, Nottinghamshire

Batting

M	I	NO	Runs	HS
257	399	34	8328	160
Ave	50	100	ct/st	
22.81	33	13	180	

Bowling

Runs	Wkts	Av	BB	5wI	10wM
7926	436	18.17	8-64	17	3

Best Performances
160 v. Sussex, Hove, 1887
8-64 v. Gloucestershire, Cheltenham College, 1888

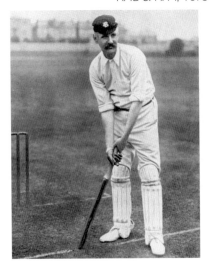

W.G. Grace once remarked that William Barnes had a remarkable faculty for getting out of scrapes. Billy Barnes did indeed become embroiled in a fair number of incidents on and off the field but he was also one of the great cricketers of his day, for a time the most capped Nottinghamshire player with 21 Test appearances to his name. According to Ashley-Cooper 'the county had never possessed a greater all-round player'.

Barnes was initially selected for his middle-order batting but in 1877, he became a regular first-change medium-pace bowler, heading the county's bowling averages in 1885 with a total of 57 wickets, his best return for the county. 1888 saw him record his best match figures of 13-89 against Gloucestershire, which included a career-best 8-64.

A tall, powerfully-built man, just over 6ft tall and weighing over 12st, he was a hard-hitting and adventurous batsman. He was often accused of throwing his wicket away, becoming impatient to keep the score moving. E.V. Lucas, on being asked which innings he would like to see again, said, 'Barney at his most reckless.' Described as the best professional batsman in England in 1880, he topped the Nottinghamshire averages and became the first Nottinghamshire batsman to score over 1,000 runs in a season in all first-class matches. Altogether he hit 13 of his 21 hundreds for the county, his highest innings being 160 against Sussex at Hove in 1887. In all games, he was to reach 1,000 runs on five occasions. He was involved in an impressive number of large partnerships, participating in seven county-record stands. The highest was 289 for the second wicket with Shrewsbury in 1882 against Surrey, then the highest partnership for any wicket in county cricket.

He remained a regular member of the England side throughout the 1880s, touring Australia on three occasions, finishing top of the tour batting averages on one occasion and twice heading the bowling averages. He had his share of controversy – in the Sydney Test of 1884/85, having taken offence at not being asked to bowl in the first innings, he refused to bowl in the second, arguably costing England the match. On the following tour, a pre-match scuffle with the Australian captain, McDonnell, resulted in a misdirected Barnes punch which hit a wall, ruling him out of most of the remaining tour matches.

He also proved a difficult handful for the Nottinghamshire committee, several times trying its patience with lateness, unruly behaviour and being the worst for drink. The committee had the last word, dispensing with his services immediately after his benefit in 1894, refusing to change their minds despite a wave of protest. Ashley-Cooper, highly sympathetic to Barnes, wrote 'Few men loved the game more ... he played simply because he loved cricket'.

13

Fred Barratt

RHB & RF, 1914-31

Born: 12 April 1894, Annesley, Nottinghamshire
Died: 29 January 1947, Nottingham

Batting

M	I	NO	Runs	HS
353	441	48	6101	139*
Ave	50	100	ct/st	
15.52	23	2	166	

Bowling

Runs	Wkts	Av	BB	5wI	10wM
26299	1176	22.36	8-26	67	11

Best Performances

139* v. Warwickshire, Coventry, 1928
8-26 v. Glamorgan, Cardiff Arms Park, 1922

Fred Barratt, another product of the North Nottinghamshire coalfield, a twenty year old with an impressive physique, standing over 6ft and weighing 14st, made his debut against the MCC at Lord's in the opening game of the 1914 season and returned the best-ever figures by a Notts debutant, 8-91, in MCC's first innings. He went on to claim 115 wickets in his first season, one of only eleven bowlers to have achieved this feat in the first-class game. Although being badly gassed in the closing months of the First World War, he returned to become an automatic choice, missing games only through injury or illness until his final season in 1931.

Barratt's height and strength, rather than technique, undoubtedly contributed to his ability to generate pace and to make the ball lift sharply on occasions. Later acquiring the ability to bowl the in-swinger, he proved a difficult bowler to face on a hard wicket. He became one of the county's most consistent bowlers, taking fifty or more wickets in thirteen consecutive seasons from 1914 to 1930. He was to take a hundred wickets in a season on five occasions, topping the Notts bowling averages three times and claiming most wickets in 1914 and 1929. He is still the sixth-highest wicket-taker in the county's history. His best figures were 8-28 against Glamorgan in 1922, seven of his victims being clean-bowled.

Barratt was also one of the great big-hitters of the game, striking three consecutive sixes off Wilfred Rhodes in 1919, a feat he repeated against Jupp of Northamptonshire in 1928. He

is credited with making one of the longest hits on the Trent Bridge ground, hitting the ball clean over Parr's Tree against Essex in 1923. However, he was not a slogger, his forte being the straight drive between mid-on and mid-off. Both his centuries were hard-hitting affairs. His 139* against Warwickshire took 84 minutes, including 7 sixes and 18 fours whilst his 110* against Glamorgan included 5 sixes and 12 fours. He equalled his record of 7 sixes in an innings the following summer, his unbeaten 90 against Middlesex being described as one of the best hitting displays of the season. In that same year, he struck 39 sixes, having hit 46 in 1928, the second highest number in an English season at that time.

By the late twenties, he could rightly be classed as an all-rounder, a description underlined by the double in 1928, his benefit year. The culmination of his career came in 1929 when he played a major role in the county winning the County Championship, taking over one hundred wickets for a second consecutive season and scoring over 600 runs. He was selected to play against South Africa at Old Trafford, and he appeared in all four Tests against New Zealand in 1929/30.

A great servant for the county, the combination of fast bowling and fast scoring made him one of the side's most popular and entertaining players in the twenties. He was also a professional footballer, appearing as a full-back for Aston Villa and Sheffield Wednesday.

Darren John Bicknell

LHB & LM, 2000-

Born: 24 June 1967, Guildford, Surrey

Batting

M	I	NO	Runs	HS
45	80	3	2642	180*
57	54	5	1923	117*
Ave	50	100	ct/st	
34.31	7	7	16	
39.24	16	3	15	

Bowling

Runs	Wkts	Av	BB	5wI	10wM
0	0	-	-	-	-
6	0	-	-	-	-

Best Performances

180* v. Warwickshire, Birmingham, 2000
117* v. Warwickshire, Nottingham, 2001

After a disastrous 1999 season, in which the county finished in seventeenth place, Clive Rice sought out more experienced players to bring along those promising young players that had survived a vigourous clear-out. With no settled opening pair, the acquisition of the Surrey left-hand opening batsman, Darren Bicknell, was an ideal signing. A career average of almost forty, higher than any of the current Nottinghamshire batsmen, 32 first-class hundreds, three tours with the England A side and centuries in each of the limited-overs competitions all made a convincing case, as did the memory of a career-best 235* at Trent Bridge in 1994, the longest innings in county cricket, taking 638 minutes.

In the three seasons that Bicknell has been with the county, he has lived up to the expectations placed upon him, participating in a number of record achievements. Virtually an ever-present as an opening batsman in Championship matches, he has averaged over thirty in all three seasons and hit seven hundreds. His highest innings of 180*, his maiden hundred for the county in 502 minutes, underlined his ability to occupy the crease for long periods. He also wrote himself into the county's record books, his unbroken first-wicket partnership of 406 with Welton against Warwickshire

being the first-ever 400-run partnership for Nottinghamshire, as well as being the highest unbeaten partnership in the Championship. It also gave Bicknell a unique batting record – the only English batsman to have figured in two partnerships of over 400 runs. In addition, he shared another huge stand of 316 with Pieterson against division leaders Middlesex in 2002.

His ability to pace an innings was seen at its best in his innings of 167 against Warwickshire in 2001, when he occupied the crease until the 400-run target for bonus points had almost been reached. In the same year, his 104 out of the first 259 runs assisted the county in establishing a county record of a highest winning second innings total of 461-3. He has been equally successful in limited-overs cricket, showing himself capable of scoring quick runs when necessary. Scoring over 500 runs twice in the National League, he has already hit centuries in both that division and in the Benson & Hedges competition. He won a second consecutive Gold Award for his 117* in the 2001 quarter-final, becoming only the second player to score 1,000 runs in both the Championship and in one-day cricket in the same season. His first-wicket partnership with Gallian of 196 in 2000 against Surrey in the National League is also a county record. His consistency, experience and professionalism should serve the county well in their introduction to Division One cricket in 2003.

Samuel Biddulph
RHB & WK, 1862-75

Born: 23 December 1840, Hyson Green,
 Nottingham
Died: 7 March 1876, Nottingham

Batting

M	I	NO	Runs	HS
76	118	17	983	54
Ave	50	100	ct/st	
9.73	1	-	64/52	

Best Performances
54 v. Kent, Nottingham, 1869

Samuel (far right of picture) 'Biddy' Biddulph's career for Nottinghamshire was sandwiched between two highly extrovert wicketkeepers, 'Mad' Charlie Brown and Mordecai Sherwin, so as a quiet, unobtrusive 'keeper he has attracted far less attention than his two counterparts. Alfred Shaw claimed that Biddulph took his deliveries better than anyone else could and in his opinion was the first wicketkeeper to dispense with a longstop. It was generally accepted that he was one of the most efficient stumpers of his day, Sutton remarking that 'for quickness of sight, execution and indomitable courage, he perhaps stands second to none in the cricketing world.'

A local cricketer, in 1861, aged twenty, he appeared for XXII Colts against Nottinghamshire, an innovation by the county to discover new talent. Recognition of his talents quickly led to an appearance for the All-England XI, selection for a Colts side against MCC at Lord's, when he claimed five victims in the match, and a county debut against Cambridgeshire, 'keeping to an excellent Nottinghamshire attack of Jackson, Wootton, Tinley and Grundy. Still in his debut year, he was selected for the Players against the Gentlemen at Lord's and for England against Surrey at The Oval. These two appearances in his debut season at the premier grounds in London led to an engagement on the Lord's ground staff, a position he was to hold until the end of his cricketing career. In the

same year, he became the established Nottinghamshire 'keeper, going on to make 76 appearances, missing only 3 of the county's next 36 fixtures.

Although selected essentially for his wicket-keeping ability, many 'keepers of the time being batsmen who also kept wicket, he was also a hard-hitting batsman, his highest innings for Nottinghamshire being 54 against Kent in 1869 at Trent Bridge, when he added 110 with Bignall for the seventh wicket. He was equally useful in a crisis, being invaluable in steering Notts to a one-wicket victory against Surrey in 1874 at The Oval, when with thirteen still required for victory and his partner, J.C. Shaw, one of the county's worst batsmen, Biddulph won the match with five 'well-placed hits ... They were accompanied from the wicket by an excited, roaring, applauding crowd of at least 2,000 strong.'

In 1865, he proved to be the leading 'keeper in England, claiming 31 dismissals, and subsequently finished second to Pooley on four occasions in 1868, 1870, 1871 and 1874. In the latter year, he achieved his best performance for Notts, claiming six dismissals in the match against Surrey at Trent Bridge, including four in the second innings, his performance described in *Bell's Life* as 'simply grand'. This was also the year he claimed his highest number of victims in a season in all games, 32, this also being his most successful for Notts, when he recorded 16 victims. Sadly, it was to be his last full season for the county for within eighteen months he had died of a kidney complaint at the age of only thirty-five. Apart from his Nottinghamshire appearances, he also played regularly for MCC and for the North against the South.

Born: 8 January 1842, Chilwell, Nottinghamshire
Died: 19 September 1898, Nottingham

Batting

M	I	NO	Runs	HS
60	102	10	1895	116*
Ave	50	100	ct/st	
20.59	4	1	17	

Bowling

Runs	Wkts	Av	BB	5wI	10wM
40	0	-	-	-	-

Best Performances
116* v. Kent, Tunbridge Wells, 1869

Thomas Bignall initially made his mark in the pre-season fixture between Colts and the Nottinghamshire XI in 1862 when, opening the bowling, he produced a stunning analysis of 8-20 as Nottinghamshire were dismissed for 55. However, as Notts possessed in Jackson, Wootton and Grundy three of the best bowlers in the country, his services as a fast, round-arm bowler were not required. In the event, he was hardly ever to bowl a ball for Nottinghamshire and ended his first-class cricket career with only one wicket to his credit. However, at Lords on 1 June 1863 for a Colts XI against the MCC when facing Grundy and Wootton, he top-scored in the first innings with 27 out of 61, the only double figures of the innings, and reached 16 in the second, a score only bettered by one other batsman. A coveted place on the Lord's ground staff followed and within a week he was appearing for the MCC against Sussex at Lord's, again impressing with a top score of 49 against James Lillywhite and Wisden. Another good performance for the Players against the Gentlemen at Lord's was enough to gain him a place in the Nottinghamshire side later in the season against Yorkshire.

After such a promising first season, it would have seemed that the young twenty-two-year-old batsman would secure an automatic place in the Nottinghamshire side but after two useful seasons, he was to make no appearances in the next two years until the final match of 1868, it being noted in *Scores and Biographies* that he

'believed he had lost his play'. The game against Surrey was to resurrect Bignall's career, for he top-scored in both innings with 30 and 97, just three runs short of becoming the first batsman to reach three figures in an important game at Trent Bridge. He was to remain an ever-present for the next five seasons, missing only 3 games out of his final 44 possible appearances, before retiring at the end of the 1874 season.

The highlight of his career came in 1869, the first year of his revived career, when he struck an unbeaten 116* against Kent at Tunbridge Wells, the only hundred of his first-class career. Made out of 191, it included 3 sixes, earning him a presentation of £5. It was described in *Wisden* as 'praiseworthy for skilled defence as for brilliant hitting', his leg-hitting 'pronounced by good judges to have been equal to George Parr's in George's best days'.

In 1871, he again came close to scoring the first hundred at Trent Bridge, being dismissed for 96 in Nottinghamshire's first innings against Gloucestershire in what was an historic match, W.G. Grace's first appearance at Trent Bridge. This proved to be Bignall's best season, his 302 runs at 33.55 being both his highest aggregate and average in any season for Notts. Still in his early thirties, he was beginning to put on weight to a considerable degree, carrying 182 pounds on a 5ft 7in frame, a factor in his retirement in 1874, although he was to make one isolated appearance for the county in 1878.

John Dennis Birch

RHB & RM, 1973-88

Born: 18 June 1955, Aspley, Nottingham

Batting

M	I	NO	Runs	HS
250	374	59	8673	125
233	199	47	3736	92
Ave	50	100	ct/st	
27.53	51	6	182	
24.57	18	-	53	

Bowling

Runs	Wkts	Av	BB	5wl	10wM
2446	50	48.92	6-64	1	-
1114	35	31.82	3-26	-	

Best Performances

125 v. Leicestershire, Nottingham, 1982
92 v. Sussex, Nottingham, 1983
6-64 v. Hampshire, Bournemouth, 1975
3-26 v. Warwickshire, Birmingham, 1988

An initial glance at John Birch's career figures might suggest that a tally of only 6 hundreds in 374 innings for the county is a rather disappointing total for a middle-order batsman, who was a regular member of the highly successful Nottinghamshire side of the 1980s. Yet he was a virtual ever-present in the 1981 and 1987 Championship sides and took part in both the 1982 Benson & Hedges Final and the 1987 NatWest Final. A local cricketer, he joined the staff in 1973 and made an unexpected first-class debut as an eighteen year old one year later when an injury to Hassan required an immediate replacement at Worcester the following day.

From 1974 to 1979, he was competing for a place with other young hopefuls, initially used as a medium-pace bowler, his only notable success being his 6-64 against Hampshire in 1975, the sole occasion he was to take five or more wickets in an innings at this level. His worth as a useful middle-order batsman began to emerge in 1979 when his aggressive approach attracted attention. A six and four in consecutive balls in the final over against Northamptonshire in 1979 secured victory and an unbeaten 94 against Yorkshire in the same year included 5 sixes. His maiden first-class hundred the following year contained 5 sixes and 9 fours.

It was during the 1981 Championship-winning year that he became a permanent member of the side and began to earn himself a reputation as a good man in a crisis. It was this versatility in the middle order, an ability to score quick runs if needed but also to occupy the crease if wickets were falling, that made him such a valuable member of the side in the 1980s. He reached 1,000 runs in both 1982 and 1983, finishing second and third in the county's batting averages, averaging about thirty in the years between the two Championship successes. As in 1981, he played an important part in the 1987 success, scoring 7 Championship fifties, several being of vital importance. His 82 in 187 minutes on a difficult pitch against Malcolm Marshall helped avoid defeat against Hampshire, and his 65 in the final game against Glamorgan, sharing a partnership of 118 with Rice, put Notts on the way to the victory which secured them the Championship.

Appointed vice-captain in 1982, he experienced only three defeats in twenty-two games when called upon to lead the side. Appointed team manager in 1991, he enjoyed a highly successful first season, Notts taking fourth place in the Championship and winning the Sunday League title for the first time. His dramatic and mysterious dismissal after only three weeks of the season, having just signed a three-year contract, finally ended his association with the county. Of one thing, there can be no doubt. His enthusiasm and his commitment to the Nottinghamshire cause were justly rewarded by the success of the county side during the years in which he played a part.

John Brian Bolus
RHB & LM, 1963-72

Born: 31 January 1934, Whitkirk, Leeds, Yorkshire

Batting

M	I	NO	Runs	HS
269	482	47	15093	202*
82	80	7	1724	100*

Ave	50	100	ct/st
34.69	83	25	124
23.61	11	1	29

Bowling

Runs	Wkts	Av	BB	5wI	10wM
400	8	50.00	2-24	-	-

Best Performances
Batting:
202* v. Glamorgan, Nottingham, 1963
100 v. Yorkshire, Middlesbrough, 1963*
Bowling:
2-24 v. West Indians, Nottingham, 1966

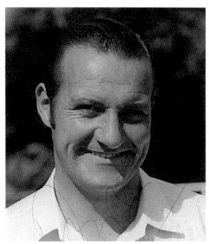

Although Bolus appeared for three counties and captained two of them, the most successful years of his first-class career were spent with Nottinghamshire. Bolus joined the county from Yorkshire, after heading the Yorkshire batting averages in 1961. Seven years with the Yorkshire club had given Nottinghamshire a highly experienced cricketer, who was to make an immediate impact in his first year with the county. In what John Arlott described as an 'I'll show 'em' act, in his first meeting with his former county in the new 65-overs competition, he carried his bat for an unbeaten 100 out of a total of 159, winning the player of the match award. He then hit 77 against Yorkshire at Trent Bridge, his first 53 out of 59 coming in 57 minutes, and followed this up with 114 in their meeting at Bradford, for which he received a standing ovation.

His 2,190 runs in all matches was the highest aggregate of the season and no batsman scored more than his 5 hundreds. A career-best 202* against Glamorgan, made out of 303 and including 5 sixes and 21 fours, was followed by a Test debut, significantly at Leeds, Bolus hitting the first ball he received from Wes Hall for four and taking ten off the over. A courageous performance in the final Test against the short-pitched bowling of Hall and Griffith earned him a place in the MCC party to India in the winter, where he appeared in all five Tests, averaging 48.87. In seven Test appearances, he never failed to reach double figures.

This remarkable first season for Nottinghamshire was the result of highly enterprising and almost carefree batting. Yet Bolus returned from India with a new approach, adopting a safer, grafting style added to an increasing use of the pads. A player who always thought deeply about his batting technique, it is unclear whether the change was a consequence of a determination to retain his Test place or perhaps to ensure a lengthy first-class career. In the event, he was omitted from the First Test at Trent Bridge and was never again selected for England.

He remained a very consistent batsman for Nottinghamshire, usually making well over 1,000 runs in all the ten seasons in which he appeared for the county. In particular, he enjoyed a very successful year in 1970, joining a select group of batsmen who have scored over 2,000 runs in a season in Nottinghamshire fixtures alone. After a spell standing in as captain for Sobers, he was appointed captain in 1972, only to find himself released by the county within a year. He was almost immediately appointed captain of Derbyshire, in 1973 scoring his usual 1,000 runs and the county's only century, not surprisingly against Yorkshire. He finally retired in 1975, having scored over 25,000 first-class runs. A great student and lover of the game, he was subsequently to become a member of England's Selection Committee.

Brian Christopher Broad
LHB & RM, 1984-92

Born: 29 September 1957, Knowle, Bristol

Batting

M	I	NO	Runs	HS
173	312	24	12386	227*
179	177	11	6262	122
Ave	50	100	ct/st	
43.00	60	31	121	
37.72	43	9	43	

Bowling

Runs	Wkts	Av	BB	5wI	10wM
260	5	52.00	2-23	-	-
198	6	33.00	2-41	-	-

Best Performances

Batting:
227* v. Kent, Tunbridge Wells, 1990
122 v. Derbyshire, Derby, 1984
Bowling:
2-23 v. Derbyshire, Derby, 1984
2-41 v. Leicestershire, Leicester, 1984

Chris Broad left Gloucestershire at the end of the 1983 season, determined to join a county which he believed would give him a greater opportunity to play Test cricket. It was an ambition he was to achieve after only ten Championship appearances for his new county. By the time he joined Notts in 1984, this tall, left-handed opening batsman had scored 1,000 runs in three of his five seasons and made 8 hundreds.

His first Nottinghamshire appearance, against Oxford University, was a foretaste of things to come. Scoring 88 and an unbeaten 108, he and Tim Robinson in their first partnership together, put on 161 and an unbroken 220 for the first wicket, only the fourth pair of Nottinghamshire opening batsmen to accomplish this feat. They were eventually to share 20 century stands out of 124 first-wicket partnerships, finishing with an average of 52.50 runs per innings, by far the best of any Nottinghamshire opening pair. Rivals for a Test place, it was suggested by Martin Johnson that 'the intense rivalry between Robinson and Broad works especially well (for Nottinghamshire) in that neither can bear to get out while the other is at the crease.'

The highpoint of his cricketing career came in the 1986/87 tour of Australia, his three centuries in the rubber assisting England to retain the Ashes. His Test career ended in 1989 when he opted to join a rebel tour of South Africa, but his Test batting average of just under forty was impressive, with 4 of his 6 centuries coming against Australia in Australia.

His Nottinghamshire figures were equally impressive, Broad reaching 1,000 runs in seven of his nine seasons, his best coming in 1990 when he scored 2,226 Championship runs, equalling the county record of 9 hundreds in a season. In the same year, he struck the only double-century of his career, his unbeaten 227 against Kent including a century before lunch on the first day, the second time he had achieved this feat. One year later, a century against Somerset gave him hundreds against seventeen different counties, with only Durham finally eluding him. His consistency in the first-class game was mirrored in limited-overs cricket, few Nottinghamshire batsmen being able to match his overall average of over 36.

Having hit two match-saving centuries against Yorkshire and Leicestershire, he was released by the new manager, Mike Hendrick. No reasonable explanation was offered, but it was to give Broad the unique record of having scored a hundred in his first and last appearance for the county. He returned to Gloucestershire, but growing problems with an arthritic hip forced him to retire in 1994. A strong personality, his career had its share of controversial moments, but his batting prowess was a vital factor in one of the most successful decades in the county's long history.

Harold James Butler
RHB & RFM, 1933-54

Born: 12 March 1913, Clifton, Nottingham
Died: 17 July 1991, Lenton, Nottingham

Batting

M	I	NO	Runs	HS
306	366	93	2870	62
Ave	50	100	ct/st	
10.51	4	-	107	

Bowling

Runs	Wkts	Av	BB	5wI	10wM
22263	919	24.22	8-15	46	6

Best Performances
Batting:
62 v. Glamorgan, Swansea, 1939
Bowling:
8-15 v. Surrey, Nottingham, 1937

A successful fast bowler in local cricket, Butler made his county debut in 1933, at the age of twenty, as a replacement for the injured Larwood, claiming the great Hampshire batsman Phil Mead as his first victim. Although capped the following season, it was not until 1937 that he emerged as the county's leading bowler. In that year, he achieved hat-tricks against Surrey, all his victims being clean bowled, and Leicestershire. The Surrey game brought him a career-best 8-15, the best eight-wicket analysis by a Nottinghamshire bowler since 1862, especially commendable as Larwood and Voce both bowled in the same innings. A third hat-trick, equalling Alfred Shaw's county record, followed in 1939, again without assistance from the field. He began 1938 in sensational style, taking 36 wickets at 17.25 apiece by mid-June, only to be struck down by appendicitis, which brought his season to an end. He was again the county's leading bowler in 1939, for the first time taking over 100 wickets at an average of 22.59.

After the war, he became the mainstay of the county attack, being the side's leading bowler in the first five post-war seasons and again in 1952, in his thirty-ninth year, despite being over-bowled and lacking support. Always heavily built, he was now becoming overweight. His unathletic appearance, added to a rather flat-footed run-up, did not inspire confidence in his ability as a fast bowler of quality, but he possessed genuine pace with an excellent delivery and a talent for moving the ball both ways. With the selectors desperate to discover a fast opening attack in the immediate post-war years, an excellent season in 1947, in which he took 100 wickets for the second time and bowled almost 1,000 overs, saw him chosen for the Fourth Test at Headingley against South Africa, where he made an impressive debut, taking seven wickets in the match. Hopes that England had found a genuine pace bowler, even in the short term, were dashed by injury, which prevented him playing in the Fifth Test. Although chosen to tour the West Indies in the winter, a leg-strain in the opening game and the return of malaria, a legacy of his war service, allowed him only one further Test appearance. His age, his proneness to injury and illness made him too much of a gamble for future Test selection, even though others were tried and failed against Australia in 1948.

He continued to play for Nottinghamshire until 1954, although three of those seasons were curtailed by injury. His final and only game in 1954 lasted only seven overs, when after dislocating a shoulder he retired on medical advice. Ironically, it came at the point when the county had taken steps to produce more bowler-friendly pitches and employ the services of a world-class spinner, Bruce Dooland. Harold Butler was a great servant for the county when its fortunes were at their lowest ebb. His courage, stamina and popularity were recognised by the crowd of 20,000 who turned up on the first day of his benefit match in 1950.

Christopher Lance Cairns
RHB & RFM, 1988-

Born: 13 June 1970, Picton, Malborough, New Zealand

Batting

M	I	NO	Runs	HS
79	125	15	4309	115
79	65	11	2073	126*
Ave	50	100	ct/st	
39.17	29	5	34	
38.38	12	2	22	

Bowling

Runs	Wkts	Av	BB	5wl	10wM
6529	226	28.88	8-47	9	1
2591	116	22.33	6-52	2	-

Best Performances

115 v. Middlesex, Lord's, 1995
126* v. Surrey, The Oval, 1993
8-47 v. Sussex, Arundel, 1995
6-52 v. Kent, Nottingham, 1993

Within one year of the departure of the great New Zealander all-rounder Richard Hadlee, Nottinghamshire gave a first opportunity to the seventeen-year-old Chris Cairns in 1988. A member of the New Zealand Under-19 World Cup team in Australia in 1987/88, he finished as the fourth most successful bowler in the tournament. Awarded a cricket scholarship, he was to play in only a handful of games for Nottinghamshire in 1988 and 1989.

His growing reputation over the next few years, being described in some quarters as one of the most exciting all-rounders in the world, persuaded Nottinghamshire to offer him a contract as their overseas player in 1992. This was a bold move that necessitated the departure of the highly popular and equally successful Franklyn Stephenson. Many felt that he, together with new signing Chris Lewis, would revive the glories of the Hadlee-Rice era.

Cairns became a consistent member of the team, playing in 67 out of 73 Championship games. Twice he was to head the county's bowling averages, taking over fifty wickets in three of his four seasons. His best season with the ball was 1995 when his 52 wickets cost only 19.90 apiece, a performance which placed him sixth in the national bowling averages. Against Sussex at Arundel, he returned career-best match and innings figures, 15-83 and 8-47 respectively, the former the best return by any bowler that summer. His batting was both exhilarating and consistent. His 5 hundreds were usually rapid affairs and laced with boundaries. His century against

Cambridge University in 1995 took only 76 minutes and 65 balls and included 7 sixes and 7 fours, the fastest hundred of the season. His initial Championship hundred for Nottinghamshire in 1993, at Trent Bridge against Lancashire, took only 119 balls and included 5 sixes and 10 fours, whilst his 6-70 in the same match, at that time his best innings figures for the county, underlined his all-round contribution to the side. In the same vein, his unbeaten 107 against Gloucestershire at Worksop included 3 sixes and 17 fours.

Less well known was his consistently high percentage of innings of over fifty, an extremely useful asset for a middle-order all-rounder. Whilst he was to pass 1,000 runs in only one season, 1995, he scored well over 900 in the other three, averaging over forty in these four seasons. Since last playing for the county in 1996, Cairns has fulfilled all his potential as a Test player. One of *Wisden's* Five Cricketers of the Year in 2000, he was spoken of as the game's pre-eminent all-rounder. Nottinghamshire again signed him as their overseas player on a two-year contract in 2002, but an injury sustained during England's winter tour of New Zealand prevented him appearing. Hopes now rest on a complete recovery in time for the 2003 English season.

Born: 21 May 1893, Mickleham, Surrey
Died: 7 February 1963, West Witton, Yorkshire

Batting

M	I	NO	Runs	HS
416	630	40	18855	206
Ave	50	100	ct/st	
31.95	84	43	367	

Bowling

Runs	Wkts	Av	BB	5wl	10wM
1150	31	37.09	3-14	-	-

Best Performances

206 v. Leicestershire, Aylestone Road, Leicester, 1925
3-14 v. Derbyshire, Nottingham, 1920

Arthur Carr was the most successful as well as one of the most popular Nottinghamshire captains, leading the county in 397 games, over a hundred more than any other, winning 171 matches and losing only 60. In the nineteen seasons from 1919 to 1934, Nottinghamshire finished in fourth place or above on ten occasions, being runners-up three times and winning the Championship in 1929. His uncompromising and aggressive approach to the game, both on and off the field, was also to bring him into conflict with the cricket authorities at both national and local level, eventually contributing to the end of his first-class career with the county.

His precocious talent earned him a place in the county Second XI at the age of fifteen, for whom he scored an unbeaten 102*, adding 275 for the first wicket with James Iremonger. Within a year, whilst still at Sherborne, he was making his first-class debut, aged 17 years and 96 days, at that time the youngest to appear in a Championship match for the county. His self-confident and positive approach to batting was soon in evidence in 1913, when he struck 169 against Leicestershire in 180 minutes, being involved in a third-wicket partnership of 333.

He was appointed full-time captain after the First World War. Carr stated in his book *Cricket with the Lid Off* that he had heard that the players did not 'want any bloody amateurs in the side', a comment which probably had an ele-

ment of truth in it, considering the number of experienced, tough, North Nottinghamshire professionals in the team. Carr was soon to win them over by his leadership, his own belligerent batting style and his outstanding ability as a close-in fielder. He quickly established a reputation as a dangerous batsman, who could turn a game by powerful and aggressive hitting. His trademark was the straight drive, especially off the faster bowlers, some claiming there was no better driver in the game at that time. His explosive batting brought him two of the fastest hundreds for the county; he took only 48 minutes to reach three figures against Sussex in 1925 and 60 minutes against Northamptonshire in 1928. He was twice to score a hundred runs before lunch on the third day of a match and in 1925 struck 48 sixes – a national record. The very nature of his batting did not make for consistency, although he still scored over 1,000 runs in eleven seasons. In 1925 he enjoyed his most successful season with the bat, hitting 8 hundreds in all, scoring over 2,300 runs at an average of over fifty and achieving a career-best 206 against Leicestershire, the second of his first-class double hundreds. His courageous close fielding earned him 25 or more catches in a season for the county on five occasions, his best being 31 in the Championship year. Only two other

Arthur Carr, the only Nottinghamshire captain to lead England at Trent Bridge.

Nottinghamshire players have bettered his final tally of 367 catches.

His Test career began in South Africa, where he appeared in all five Tests in 1922/23, subsequently being chosen as one of *Wisden's* Five Cricketers of the Year. His enterprising and aggressive captaincy of the Nottinghamshire side persuaded the selectors to choose him to lead the England side in 1926 against the Australians. It was to prove a personally disappointing series for Carr. Becoming the first Nottinghamshire player to lead England on his home ground, rain reduced the match to a mere 50 minutes. Carr then took a calculated risk in the Third Test at Leeds, putting the Australians in. Australia lost a wicket to the first ball of the match, only for Carr himself to drop Macartney off the fourth, the Australian going on to make a century before lunch. His captaincy now under pressure, he was only able to appear on the first day in the Fourth Test before tonsillitis forced him out of the match. Incredibly, he had played only one innings in four Tests. With the regain-ing of the Ashes dependent on the Fifth Test, the decision was taken to replace him. Correct or not, the manner in which it was done reflected little credit on the selectors. Their insistence that he had offered to stand down was emphatically denied by Carr. After his removal from the England captaincy in 1926, he was subsequently cheered all the way to the wicket at Old Trafford. Cardus commented that 'It is not the many but the few that have deposed him from the England captaincy.' He was subsequently to captain England twice more in 1929.

Having led the county to the Championship title in 1929, he now became embroiled in the controversial employment of fast-leg theory by Larwood and Voce against other county sides, later asserting he had played a key role in its use in the Bodyline series of 1932/33 and fully supporting the actions of his fast bowlers. Matters came to a head in the county's fixture against the Australians in 1934 when Voce, bowling leg-theory, took 8-66 in the first innings, but he was declared unfit to bowl in the second. Carr, although not captaining the side after suffering a heart attack earlier in the season, publicly stated that Voce was fit and that the committee had caved in to pressure from the Australians and others. The committee, already worried that a number of counties were unwilling to renew their fixtures with Nottinghamshire, decided to replace him. After a major confrontation between the committee and the membership, Carr was not reinstated but did indicate that he wished to continue playing. He never again appeared for Nottinghamshire.

All the controversy surrounding Carr at both county and Test level overshadowed his undoubted prowess as a fine cricketer and captain. It was once said that he was a captain 'who always thinks more of his team than he does of himself'. Highly respected by his players, he was an extremely popular cricketer, whom many felt had been let down by the cricketing establishment at all levels.

William Clarke
RHB & RS (under-arm), 1826-55

Born: 24 December 1798, Nottingham
Died: 25 August 1856, Wandsworth, Surrey

Batting

M	I	NO	Runs	HS
41	71	3	786	75
Ave	50	100	ct/st	
11.55	3	-	22	

Bowling

Runs	Wkts	Av	BB	5wl	10wM
1256	134	9.37	9-29	18	-

Best Performances
75 v. Gentlemen of Nottinghamshire,
   Nottingham, 1842
9-29 v. Kent, Nottingham, 1845

William Clarke's place in the annals of cricket is assured by two significant contributions to the game. In 1838 he laid out Trent Bridge Cricket Ground, which became not only the future home of Nottinghamshire cricket but one of the great Test match grounds. He was also the founder, in 1846, of the first professional travelling side, the All-England XI, bringing to every corner of England the greatest players of the day. It provided a major stimulus to the development and spread of cricket throughout the country, giving good rewards to the leading players of the day and providing the opportunity for ambitious local cricketers to test their skills against the best, with the possibility of being recruited by Clarke if they proved worthy. These achievements have, however, overshadowed his cricketing career as an outstanding slow under-arm bowler.

His business acumen had led him to lay out the Trent Bridge ground; for the first time, spectators were asked to pay for the privilege of watching Nottinghamshire cricket. For similar commercial reasons, he moved to London to join the MCC in 1846, allowing him to play in all the important matches of the season and also to put together his All-England XI. Although playing for the Nottingham club from the age of seventeen in 1816 and later becoming its captain, he was little known outside the county until that year. Only then, at the age of forty-seven, after thirty seasons in the game, did he make his debut for the Players against the Gentlemen.

Clarke appeared in the Nottingham club's first important fixture against Sheffield and Leicester at Sheffield in July 1826 and subsequently appeared in 41 out of a possible 48 Nottinghamshire fixtures between 1826 and 1855. However, his involvement with the AEE and MCC led to a virtual neglect of the Nottinghamshire club, with no matches being organised in 1846, 1848 and 1849. Clarke himself made no appearances between 1846 and 1850 and even organised two AEE games which clashed with Nottinghamshire fixtures. Only when his personal career and the AEE were flourishing did Clarke again renew his interest in the county, continuing to lead the side and run the county's affairs until his retirement. He remained fully in control of both the Nottinghamshire club and the AEE, selecting the various England XIs and the North against the South, as well as playing almost up to the time of his death.

He began mainly as a batsman, often opening the innings, his 65 in 1834 being the highest innings by a Nottinghamshire player at that time, but the loss of a right eye in an accident

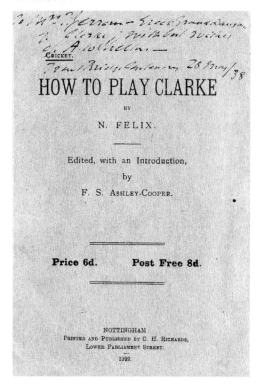

CRICKET.

HOW TO PLAY CLARKE

BY

N. FELIX.

Edited, with an Introduction,

by

F. S. ASHLEY-COOPER.

Price 6d.   **Post Free 8d.**

NOTTINGHAM:
PRINTED AND PUBLISHED BY C. H. RICHARDS,
LOWER PARLIAMENT STREET.
1922.

A contemporary pamphlet on how to combat one of the greatest under-arm bowlers.

headwork I should be hit out of the field.' He was correctly described as 'a crafty and fox-headed cricketer altogether'. Many of his observations on the game are as relevant today as then. 'At times it's enough to make you bite your thumbs to see your best balls pulled and sky-rocketed about – all luck – but you must console yourself with "Ah, that won't last long".' He was also something of a sledger, 'preying on the terrors of his victims by making caustic and cocksure remarks.' Known as the 'celebrated slow bowler, 'his success was such that even a pamphlet by the renowned batsman Felix was published entitled *How to play Clarke.*'

He twice claimed nine wickets in an innings for Nottinghamshire, his 9-29 against Kent at Trent Bridge in 1845 bringing him match figures of 16-67, nine of his victims being clean-bowled. His nine first-innings wickets included three of the leading batsmen in England: Fuller Pitch, Alfred Mynn and Felix in quick succession, the latter two being clean-bowled for nought. It is claimed that he took 2,327 wickets between 1848 and 1854, although the majority of these would have come from matches involving playing against odds. Even so, he was to take wickets in all the important fixtures of the day, sharing all twenty wickets with William Lillywhite against the Gentlemen in 1847, taking 15 for 98 for the North against the South and achieving a hat-trick for England against Kent. He appeared for the last time in 1855, aged 56 years 237 days, still the oldest player to represent the county. Ashley-Cooper devoted a whole chapter to William Clarke in his *Nottinghamshire Cricket and Cricketers*, published in 1923, writing that 'In the whole period of 150 years covered by the history of cricket in Nottinghamshire, no figure stands out more prominently than that of William Clarke, the celebrated slow bowler.' He remains a typical representative of his age, a Victorian entrepreneur who rose from humble origins to make money through a new approach or idea.

playing fives led him to concentrate on slow under-arm bowling. This type of bowling had become unfashionable; round-arm had become the norm, a factor which some claimed contributed to his future success. More probably, he obtained many of his wickets because batsmen underestimated his style of bowling, believing they could hit it out of the ground. Clarke did not just bowl under-arm lobs but also made the ball spin sharply from leg and occasionally threw in a well-disguised fast ball, often a full-pitcher which hit the top of the stumps. Caffyn commented that 'it was the fear of this ball, which made you hesitate to go out and hit the slow ones. I really think that this was the bottom of his success.' He was extremely accurate, according to Richard Daft, seldom bowling two balls alike, being able to vary his pace and pitch in a wonderful manner. He was also one of the first examples of a bowler who studied and noted the weak points of a batsman and set his field accordingly. Clarke himself remarked, 'Without

Born: 25 October 1924, West Bridgford, Nottingham

Batting

M	I	NO	Runs	HS
236	400	17	9991	192
Ave	**50**	**100**	**ct/st**	
26.03	49	11	164	

Bowling

Runs	Wkts	Av	BB	5wI	10wM
133	0	-	-	-	-

Best Performances

192 v. Hampshire, Nottingham, 1952

Born within half a mile of Trent Bridge and still living nearby, John Clay was to play all his 236 first-class innings for Nottinghamshire. He was a correct batsman with an orthodox style, not noted for being a great stroke player, but one who was prepared to graft for his runs and not give his wicket away lightly. In a side, which for many years contained batsmen of the calibre of Keeton, Simpson, Hardstaff and Cyril Poole, he fulfilled an important supporting role. After a season of Second XI cricket, he made his first-class debut against Leicestershire at Trent Bridge in 1948. His opportunity to break into the First XI came in 1951 as the county searched for a new permanent opening pair to replace the long-lived Keeton-Harris combination. The fifth opener to be tried, he proved an immediate success with his maiden first-class hundred against Somerset at Trent Bridge, his 112 coming in his sixteenth first-class appearance. Although subsequently giving way to Simpson and Keeton as an opening batsman, he completed a second hundred against Derbyshire and just missed another by four runs against Worcestershire. Second to Simpson with an average of forty-four, Clay was acclaimed in the *Playfair Cricket Annual* as the county's most promising recruit.

For the next four seasons, Clay was an established member of the team, consistently reaching 1,000 runs, and by mid-1953 he had become one of the team's regular opening batsmen, sharing in several century opening partnerships with Simpson. His ability to occupy the crease was seen in his career-best 192 against Hampshire at

Trent Bridge in 1952, when he batted for seven and a half hours. After 1955 he was to appear less regularly in the side, especially after the advent of Norman Hill as opener, although he again scored 1,000 runs in 1957. He continued to play for the Second XI, filling in when needed until 1961 when Simpson's resignation as the captain led him, as the county's senior professional, to take over; he was the first professional captain of the side since Arthur Shrewsbury. His final first-class season must have generated mixed feelings, for whilst the county finished last in the table, he enjoyed his best season with the bat, scoring 1,497 in all games, his most productive year. Assuming the role of opener once more, he finished with a flourish of runs in the second half of the season, making a century in his penultimate first-class match. His sporting approach to the captaincy in this year earned a special comment in *Wisden*. One aspect of his game, which is often overlooked, was his skill as a slip fielder; Clay's 33 catches in 1955 being the highest number for the county since 1929. His 6 catches in an innings against Derbyshire in 1957 remains a county record. He continued to lead the Second XI for another seven seasons and he still retains a keen interest in the game. A modest man, he once described himself as an 'ordinary player'. A better description would be of a man who loved the game and understood the great privilege of representing his county.

Kevin Edwin Cooper
LHB & RFM, 1976-92

Born: 27 December 1957, Sutton-in-Ashfield, Nottinghamshire

Batting

M	I	NO	Runs	HS
272	281	67	2141	46
245	86	33	405	31
Ave	50	100	ct/st	
10.00	-	-	84	
7.64	-	-	45	

Bowling

Runs	Wkts	Av	BB	5wI	10wM
19304	711	27.15	8-44	25	1
7639	241	31.69	4-9	-	

Best Performances

46 v. Middlesex, Nottingham, 1985
31 v. Gloucestershire, Nottingham, 1984
8-44 v. Middlesex, Lord's, 1984
4-9 v. Yorkshire, Nottingham, 1989

Kevin Cooper made his first-class debut against Cambridge University in 1976, aged 18 years and 182 days, making a favourable first impression with 4-26 off 17 overs in the first innings and eight wickets in the match, the best start by a local debutant since Bill Voce in 1927. It was an early indication of what was to become one of his greatest assets, an ability to bowl an accurate line and length. Possessing an easy action, a bowler of aggravating length and capable of long, accurate spells, he came to be an essential part of the county's attack. A Championship debut followed, his first victim being the Indian Test batsman, Majid Khan. Coupled with some useful performances in the Sunday League, Cooper was hailed in some quarters as the find of the season.

His early career until 1980 was one of stops and starts, in part the consequence of injury, something which was to interrupt his subsequent career. Capped in 1980, and still only twenty-three years of age, he became an integral part of the Nottinghamshire attack, carrying the burden of stock bowler during the Hadlee-Rice years. Between 1982 and 1985, he bowled well over 500 overs in each season, the most by any of the county seamers in three of those years. During this time he returned career-best figures of 8-44 against Middlesex at Lord's. A motoring accident and other injuries again curtailed his contribution in both 1986 and 1987, forcing him to miss the NatWest Final.

With the departure of Hadlee and Rice, 1988 was a crucial year with competition from Andy Pick and the arrival of Franklyn Stephenson. To complicate matters, Cooper had suffered a broken leg playing football during the winter. He rose to the challenge magnificently, being ever-present in the Championship for the only time in his career. Opening with the new ball for the first time on a regular basis, he went on to secure 101 wickets at a cost of only 21.57 apiece, the first Nottinghamshire-born bowler to achieve this since Arthur Jepson in 1947. He and Stephenson, both of whom bowled more overs than any other bowler in the country, became the first pair of county bowlers since 1969 to take over a hundred wickets. Previously underrated, Cooper was at last recognised as one of the best swing and seam bowlers in the country. In the following two seasons, he again bowled more overs than any other Nottinghamshire bowler, in 1989 taking ten wickets in a match for the only time.

Requiring major back surgery in 1991, he was released at the close of the 1992 season having played little or no cricket in either year. He appeared for Gloucestershire for a further four years and still continues to perform with success in Minor Counties cricket. During his seventeen seasons, approximately another fifteen bowlers of a similar type appeared for the county. None took as many wickets and few returned a better bowling average.

John Cotton
RHB & RFM, 1958-64

Born: 7 July 1940, Newstead, Nottinghamshire

Batting

M	I	NO	Runs	HS
138	194	67	1047	58
2	2	0	6	6
Ave	50	100	ct/st	
8.24	1	-	40	
3.00	-	-	-	

Bowling

Runs	Wkts	Av	BB	5wI	10wM
10368	400	25.92	7-73	15	1
81	3	27.00	3-49	-	-

Best Performances
58 v. Hampshire, Nottingham, 1960
6 v. Somerset, Taunton, 1964
7-73 v. Somerset, Nottingham, 1959
3-49 v. Somerset, Taunton, 1964

The years in which John Cotton appeared for the county were not those that any young player would have chosen when embarking upon a first-class cricket career. In six of his seven seasons with the county, Nottinghamshire were to finish fifteenth or lower in the Championship, winning only 33 out of 211 games. It was a time when bowlers came and went with regularity. Cotton's own debut was typical of the desperate straits into which the county had fallen. His potential as a young fast bowler was recognised when he joined the staff in 1956, at a mere fifteen years of age. Initial success with the introduction of a number of young players in 1957, and a very promising year in the Second XI by Cotton, prompted the county to field an opening attack against Middlesex at Lord's of Cotton, aged 17 years and 181 days, the youngest bowler to have appeared in a Championship match for the county, and nineteen-year-old Paul Taylor. The latter survived for only six games but Cotton, still lacking the physique necessary for an opening bowler, was nursed sensibly, finishing with a highly creditable 44 wickets at 25.50 apiece. His first real taste of success came towards the end of the season, when in consecutive games he claimed 6-65 against Warwickshire and 5-57 against Surrey at The Oval.

Sadly, the young Cotton, still only eighteen, was to take a larger share of the bowling whilst he was still learning his trade and physically developing. In two seasons, he bowled over 700 overs, the second highest number by any Notts bowler, the price of being increasingly successful. He returned his best Nottinghamshire figures, 7-73 against Somerset in 1959, a year in which he topped the county's bowling averages. In 1960, the year in which he was capped, he claimed his best return in a season, 82 wickets at a very competitive 24.51 apiece. This included 5-69 against the visiting South Africans, when he took three wickets in four balls, and a devastating first spell of five wickets for five runs against Glamorgan, prompting speculation that he might be included in a young MCC touring party to New Zealand in the following winter. The year 1960 proved to be the high watermark of his Nottinghamshire career, for injuries in the next four seasons were to limit his appearances. Even so, he finished second in the county's averages in 1961, '62 and '63, with his 65 wickets in 1963 costing only 21.98 apiece.

Released at the end of the 1964 season, still only twenty-three years of age and having taken 400 wickets in seven seasons, he proved his worth with Leicestershire, his new county. Participating in a more experienced and balanced attack, he achieved a hat-trick against Surrey and a career-best 9-29 against the Indian tourists in 1967. Although leaving the game at the early age of twenty-eight, his final career average compared favourably with many of the county's most successful bowlers.

Born: 2 November 1835, Nottingham
Died: 18 July 1900, Radcliffe-on-Trent, Nottinghamshire

Batting

M	I	NO	Runs	HS
157	261	35	6627	161
Ave	**50**	**100**	**ct/st**	
29.32	38	4	93	

Bowling

Runs	Wkts	Av	BB	5wI	10wM
829	45	18.42	6-59	2	-

Best Performances
161 v. Yorkshire, Nottingham, 1873
6-59 v. Yorkshire, Bramall Lane, Sheffield, 1872

Richard Daft dominated the Nottinghamshire batting from the mid-1860s until 1877, heading the county's batting averages for all but three seasons between 1864 and 1877. The successor to George Parr as the county's most prolific batsman, Daft was recognised as being a beautiful player to watch: 'a model of grace and execution'. He also cultivated a peculiar shot of his own: the 'dog-leg', raising his left leg and hitting the ball under it towards the leg boundary, a stroke he warned young batsman not to imitate. Christopher Martin Jenkins later observed, 'Had there been no W.G. Grace, the fame of Richard Daft would have been greater.'

He made his debut in first-class cricket in 1858, and by the end of his first season in important cricket had appeared for all of the major representative teams, as well as retaining his place in the Nottinghamshire XI. However, by 1862 Daft took the decision to limit his cricketing activities, wishing to give ample time to his business interests. He had also taken the decision to give up his amateur status and become a professional; in 1860, he became the first cricketer to appear for both Players and Gentlemen.

From 1858, he rarely missed a game for Nottinghamshire, becoming the first player to complete one hundred appearances for the county in 1876, the same year in which he became the first batsman to score over 600 runs for the county in one season. This made him Nottinghamshire's leading run-scorer, overtaking William Oscroft's aggregate of 5,237. In three consecutive years he averaged over sixty, finishing second behind W.G. Grace in the national batting averages, as he also did in 1873. Of his 4 hundreds, his 161 against Yorkshire at Trent Bridge in 1873 was at the time the highest innings for the county. His recognised ability on a difficult pitch was seen when he carried his bat for 12*, when Nottinghamshire were shot out for 48 against Lancashire at Trent Bridge in 1877.

Becoming captain in 1871, he led the county on 118 occasions until his resignation in 1880, Nottinghamshire being recognised as Champions or joint Champions six times. After a lengthy interval he was recalled in 1891, then aged fifty-five, to play against Surrey at The Oval. He was accorded a great reception by the spectators when he went out to bat.

For other teams, he was the only batsman to score a century in the fixtures between the All-England XI and the United All-England XI. He captained the Players between 1875 and 1879 and appeared in 24 games against the Gentlemen. He reached three figures on one occasion: 102 at Lord's in 1872.

He was something of a sports fanatic, participating in a wide variety of sports, including playing for Notts County FC. After retiring from cricket, he became a first-class umpire and wrote his memoirs, entitled *Kings of Cricket*. His brother C.F. Daft and two sons, H.B. Daft and R.P. Daft, also appeared for the county.

Ian Joseph Davison
RHB & RMF, 1959-66

Born: 4 October 1937, Hemel Hempstead, Hertfordshire

Batting

M	I	NO	Runs	HS
177	246	65	1641	60*
5	4	2	23	14*
Ave	50	100	ct/st	
9.06	3	-	91	
11.50	-	-	-	

Bowling

Runs	Wkts	Av	BB	5wI	10wM
15562	540	28.81	7-28	22	2
130	6	21.66	4-34	-	-

Best Performances
60* v. Sussex, Nottingham, 1962
14* v. Somerset, Taunton, 1964
7-28 v. Derbyshire, Nottingham, 1962
4-34 v. Somerset, Taunton, 1964

The 1958 season saw Nottinghamshire not only finish last in the Championship but, having lost Dooland in 1957, the club now suffered the departure of four more bowlers – Walker, Smales, Goonesena and Harvey – leaving behind the evergreen forty-three-year-old Jepson and the promising seventeen-year-old John Cotton. A frantic search for replacements led the signing by special registration of Ian Davison, a right-arm fast-medium bowler, who had first appeared for Bedfordshire aged seventeen and had proved successful in his five seasons with the minor county. Over his six seasons with the county, Davison was to take more wickets than any other bowler in the side, averaging about 67 a season in an attack that was constantly changing, and in a team which only once escaped filling one of the last three places in the Championship.

Although claiming Close and Illingworth as his first two victims against Yorkshire, Davison found it hard to adjust to the demands of Championship cricket in his initial two seasons, his wayward length often causing him to be omitted from the side. Then followed four highly successful seasons, in which he took more wickets than any other seamer in the XI, heading the bowling averages in 1962 and 1963, and

again taking the most wickets in 1964. With Cotton missing many games, allowing Davison greater opportunities, he was unfortunate to fall short of 100 wickets in 1961, having taken 87 wickets before missing the final three games of the season through injury. He continued his good form in the first half of 1962, not only hitting his highest score of 60* in his first game but following this with 5-21 and 7-28 in the next two, the latter against Derbyshire proving to be a career-best performance. By the end of June, he had taken five wickets in an innings on five occasions, for a time heading the national averages but, possibly overworked, he was to miss five of the last six fixtures.

His wholehearted approach was to pay dividends in 1963, when, reducing his pace, he became the first Nottinghamshire seamer since Jepson in 1947 to take over a hundred wickets, his 111 wickets being taken at the highly economical average of 21.92. For the first time, he took over ten wickets in a match, claiming 11-53 against Lancashire at Old Trafford. Davison's contribution was a major factor in the six victories, which lifted the county into ninth position. He again took ten wickets in a match in 1964, a career-best 13-102 against Warwickshire, with a first innings analysis of 7-68. He did less well in his final two seasons, being kept out by Corran and Forbes in 1965. After losing his place again after injury during the following season, Davison decided to leave the first-class game, returning to his former county, Bedfordshire at the relatively early age of twenty-nine.

John Auger Dixon

RHB & RM, 1882-1905

Born: 27 May 1861, Grantham, Lincolnshire
Died: 8 June 1931, The Park, Nottingham

Batting

M	I	NO	Runs	HS
235	387	24	8956	268*
Ave	50	100	ct/st	
24.67	33	13	161	

Bowling

Runs	Wkts	Av	BB	5wI	10wM
4777	172	27.77	5-28	2	-

Best Performances
268* v. Sussex, Nottingham, 1897
5-28 v. Leicestershire, Nottingham, 1900

The Dixon gates on the Bridgford Road commemorate Dixon's long service to the county club as player, captain and committee member. Although born in Lincolnshire, Dixon lived in Nottingham from the age of thirteen, being educated at the Nottingham High School. An outstanding local club cricketer with both bat and ball, he was given an early opportunity in 1882 at the age of twenty-one, but proving extremely nervous, he was not selected again that season. He made a few appearances between 1883 and 1886, achieving little in the great Nottinghamshire XI of that time, but in 1887 he gave a glimpse of his undoubted talent. When unexpectedly called up for an under-strength Notts side against MCC at Lord's at the last minute, he opened the batting, scoring 89 against a bowling attack, which included the formidable George Wootton. He cemented his place in the side with a hat-trick against Lancashire at Trent-Bridge, only the second bowler to achieve this feat for the county. He was not in truth considered as one of the county's better bowlers, his medium pace being called upon from time to time, claiming five wickets in an innings twice in his career, his best being 5-28.

Shrewsbury's absence in the 1888 season gave him greater opportunities and he ended the season at the head of the county's batting averages. Now recognised as a regular player in the side, he was offered the captaincy of the side at the start of the 1889 season; Nottinghamshire becoming the last county to give up the professional captaincy.

Dixon went on to captain Nottinghamshire in 161 games, the side just about winning as many games as it lost under his leadership. Whilst the Nottinghamshire historian Ashley-Cooper tended to praise his captaincy, there were others who felt he was ultra-cautious and rather unenterprising. In fairness, Dixon was presiding over an eleven which was in a state of flux, with many of the former great players in the final years of their careers and new players such as Tom Wass, John Gunn and A.O. Jones all in the process of establishing themselves.

Dixon continued in the side after giving up the captaincy, eventually scoring 13 centuries for the county, ending his career with a modest average of 24.67. His best year came in 1897, when he played the highest innings to date by a Nottinghamshire batsman: an unbeaten 268* against Sussex at Trent Bridge, an innings which spread over all three days of the match. He just missed a century in both innings against Kent, making 102 out of 168 and 91. It was the only season that he reached 1,000 runs for the county, joining the select company of William Gunn and Shrewsbury, the only other batsmen to have so far achieved this feat.

He continued his association with the county after his retirement, serving for forty years on the committee, becoming the first honorary life member. He was the first Nottinghamshire player to become a Test selector and was also a talented footballer, playing for Notts County and being selected for England against Wales in 1885.

Bruce Dooland
RHB & LB, 1953-57

Born: 1 November 1923, Cowandilla, Adelaide, South Australia

Died: 8 September 1980, Adelaide, South Australia

Batting

M	I	NO	Runs	HS
140	213	18	4782	115*
Ave	50	100	ct/st	
24.52	29	1	115	

Bowling

Runs	Wkts	Av	BB	5wI	10wM
14520	770	18.85	8-20	76	18

Best Performances
115* v. Sussex, Worthing, 1957
8-20 v. Worcestershire, Nottingham, 1956

Jack Fingleton, reporting on the 1953 Australian tour of England, suggested an interesting topic for his first article might be 'Why Dooland was not thought good enough for the 1948 Australian team for England'. It was a pertinent thought, for Dooland was already beginning to show in his first year with Nottinghamshire that he was a bowler of the highest class. During the five seasons he played for the county, he was to become not just a very good leg-break bowler but a great one.

It was evident from his first involvement with the game that Bruce Dooland was destined to reach the top flight. A born athlete, he was to win a cap as a baseball pitcher and later became a nine-handicap golfer. His early success on the cricket field led to the offer of a place in the South Australia side in 1940, but the refusal of his bank employers delayed the seventeen year old's first-class debut until 1945 when, after serving as a commando in the Pacific, he went on to claim a hat-trick in his fourth first-class appearance. His impressive tally of wickets brought him Test recognition against both England and India in the immediate post-war years, but competition for places was fierce. Consequently, Dooland decided to seek employment in the Lancashire League, from where he was persuaded to join the Nottinghamshire club in 1953.

As with Richard Hadlee in the 1980s, Dooland was to sharpen all his skills in the demanding programme of the county game. Having learnt his trade on the hard, bouncy wickets in Australia, he was able to make the ball break back more in English conditions. He possessed all the armoury of the traditional wrist-spinner, the leg-break as his stock ball, interspersed with the occasional googly and top-spinner. He was quick through the air and had the ability to vary his pace and flight with no apparent change in his bowling action. His height (he was 6ft tall) and high action also gave his deliveries a lift off the pitch. Above all, like many great spin bowlers, he was constantly thinking about his bowling. Having learnt the art of the top-spinner from Clarrie Grimmett, he passed his technique on to Ritchie Benaud on the 1956 Australian tour, his advice being, 'When you can bowl it well, you'll get wickets by not bowling it. The batsmen will be looking for it all the time.'

His figures for the county were phenomenal. In each of his five seasons, his lowest tally for Championship matches alone was 129 in his final season. His first two seasons brought him the most wickets by any bowler in the country, 172 in 1953 and 196 the following year. His 181 wickets for Nottinghamshire in that year shattered Richmond's record of 169 established in 1922. Such was the yardstick of his performances that his record of 150 wickets at 23.01 in 1955 was seen as comparatively disappointing, even taking into account his problems with a split spinning finger. His work rate was prodigious, his least demanding season being 1956 when he

Bruce Dooland batting – the first outstanding overseas player to play for the county.

bowled 1,198.4 overs. In 1957, he managed 1,334 overs in all matches, the most by any bowler in England, a record he also achieved in 1954.

His outstanding season was 1954 when his efforts helped Nottinghamshire to climb into fifth place in the table, their best since 1936 and which was not to be improved upon until the arrival of Sobers in 1968. At Trent Bridge he became virtually unplayable in 1954, taking ten or more wickets in a match in ten out of the thirteen games in which he played, two of them being restricted to less than one innings. He claimed eight wickets in an innings on four occasions; his best figures came against Essex when, taking eight wickets in each innings, he returned match figures of 16-83. Trevor Bailey, playing in that game, remarked that on a lovely batting wicket, this 'represented the most complete and sustained exhibition of wrist-spin I have ever witnessed'. While not keeping up this prodigious form in his remaining three seasons with the county, he still returned some remarkable analyses, such as his 8-20 against Worcestershire in 1956 after Don Kenyon had struck ten runs off his first over. His 8-42 against Lancashire in 1957 marked the eighth time that he took eight wickets in an innings for the county.

Dooland was also making important contributions with the bat, just missing the cricketer's double in his first season by 30 runs. In that year he enjoyed a fine all-round performance against Somerset, taking 7-19 in the first innings and finishing with match figures of 12-48, also hitting 98 in 80 minutes, striking 4 sixes and 8 fours. He achieved the double in 1954 and again in 1957, achieving the target in 1957 by taking 5-4 against Warwickshire. On the second occasion, he became only the third Nottinghamshire player to complete the double in county matches alone and the only cricketer that year to accomplish the double in purely Championship matches. He also recorded another fine all-round performance against Sussex, scoring his only century for the county as well as taking ten wickets in the match.

Having topped the bowling for the fourth time in five seasons and also having finished second in the county's batting averages, it was a savage blow to the county when Dooland announced he was leaving the club at the end of the 1957 season, being determined to bring up his children in Australia. In his five years, he had missed only 8 games out of the 148 played, having taken a wicket every 48 balls. It is little wonder that during his stay at Trent Bridge, the county was often referred to as 'Doolandshire'. He was to be sadly missed both as a player and as a charming, modest man.

Born: 7 December 1856, Calverton, Nottinghamshire
Died: 1 November 1926, Carlton, Nottingham

Batting

M	I	NO	Runs	HS
281	436	28	8252	173
Ave	50	100	ct/st	
20.22	39	6	144	

Bowling

Runs	Wkts	Av	BB	5wI	10wM
11712	714	16.40	8-22	33	6

Best Performances
173 v. Derbyshire, Derby, 1885
8-22 v. Gloucestershire, Clifton, 1881

All the early portents indicated that Wilfred Flowers would experience a fulfilling career in first-class cricket. Appearing for XXII Colts of England *v.* MCC at Lord's, he claimed the wicket of W.G. Grace in both innings and was applauded by the MCC XI after making 19 runs 'so promisingly'. He made his county debut, aged twenty, in 1877 and was a permanent member of the side for the next twenty seasons. He also appeared regularly for the MCC and other representative sides.

He began his career as a useful change bowler, supporting a formidable attack of Morley, Alfred Shaw and Barnes, and as a batsman capable of contributing runs lower down the order. His medium-slow off-break bowling concentrated on steadiness and accuracy, reflected in his eighteen consecutive 4-ball maidens against Sussex at Brighton in 1885. He became just as reliable as a batsman, in no way flamboyant, possessing a sound defence and capable of hitting hard when the need arose. Equally competent in the field, he proved a safe pair of hands and an excellent returner of the ball.

With consistent displays season upon season with both bat and ball, he became of the county's most successful all-rounders. He was the first Nottinghamshire player to score over 5,000 runs and take over 500 wickets for the county; he joined a select band of players who have scored over 10,000 runs and taken over 1,000 wickets in their first-class career. His most productive year was in 1894 when he scored 822 runs, also heading the county's bowling averages for the first and only time, taking 60 wickets at 16.05 apiece. Although never scoring 1,000 runs or taking 100 wickets in Nottinghamshire matches alone, he did achieve 1,000 runs in a season on two occasions, in 1883 and 1893, and twice took over 100 wickets. In 1883, he achieved the coveted double, only the third player to do so and the first professional. His best all-round match performance came against Lancashire at Old Trafford in 1893, when he hit a century and returned match figures of 11-128, the second Nottinghamshire player to reach three figures and take over ten wickets in the same match.

His first hundred for the county was his 173 in 1885 against Derbyshire at Derby, this being the highest innings of his career. He went on to make five more hundreds for the county, one in each of his last four seasons, culminating in 107 against Sussex at Trent Bridge in his final Nottinghamshire innings. His best performance was 8-23 against Gloucestershire at Clifton in 1881, the only time he was to take eight wickets in an innings for Nottinghamshire. It also brought him career-best match figures of 12-85. He was the third bowler to claim a hat-trick for the county, all clean-bowled, against Kent at Maidstone in 1888, the second hat-trick of his career.

He played in all seven Tests of the 1884/85 and 1886/87 tour of Australia and made one Test appearance in England at Lord's in 1893. He retired in 1896 but stood as a first-class umpire from 1907 to 1912.

LHB & LM, 1959-73

Born: 9 August 1936, Cross Roads, Kingston, Jamaica

Batting

M	I	NO	Runs	HS
244	319	69	3597	86
47	23	8	152	52*
Ave	50	100	ct/st	
14.38	9	-	146	
10.13	2	-	14	

Bowling

Runs	Wkts	Av	BB	5wI	10wM
17914	706	25.37	7-19	23	2
1469	59	24.89	5-23	2	-

Best Performances
86 v. Lancashire, Southport, 1961
52 v. Derbyshire, Derby, 1973*
7-19 v. Kent, Nottingham, 1966
5-23 v. Gloucestershire, Bristol, 1969

The departure of Dooland in 1957, quickly followed by the loss of Walker, Smales, Goonesena and Harvey, forced the county to find virtually a new bowling attack to avoid once again occupying seventeenth place in the table. One of these new recruits was the twenty-two-year-old left-arm slow bowler, Carlton Forbes, who had come to England in 1956 and was now playing for Middlesbrough. Although making his first-class debut in 1959 against Cambridge University, he was obliged to play in non-Championship fixtures for two years. During this period, he developed into a left-arm medium-pacer, possibly due to the arrival of Wells in 1960.

It was not, however, as a bowler that Forbes first made his mark with the county. After appearing in only three previous first-class games, he scored just over 1,000 runs for the county in 1961, reaching this objective in his final appearance of the season. He is the only Notts player to have achieved this feat in his first full season, and his average of just over twenty is the lowest average for a Notts player reaching this target. In the same season, he recorded a career-best 86 against Lancashire, a game in which he also scored an unbeaten 64*. A total of 5 of his 9 fifties were to be scored in this season.

Although he was never again to score as many runs in a season, he gradually emerged as the best bowler in the side. He topped the county's bowling averages for four consecutive seasons, taking over a hundred wickets in three of them, being the last Nottinghamshire bowler to achieve this until Richard Hadlee in 1981. His

bowling averages between 15.78 and 22.55 bear witness to his accuracy, especially as he had become the workhorse of the attack, bowling over 1,000 overs in 1965 and over 900 in each of the next two seasons. This achievement was all the more commendable as he was the only constant factor in an ever-changing attack in a side which was never out of the bottom three places in the Championship. During these years, he returned his best bowling figures, 7-19 against Kent in 1966, beating his 7-30 against Warwickshire the previous season, which included three wickets in four balls. The year 1968 at last brought some relief, with assistance from new signings Sobers and Halfyard, but it was to be his last full-scale season. Injuries in 1970 led to his virtual retirement from the first-class game, although he still continued to appear in limited-overs cricket, taking his second haul of five wickets in an innings in 1973 in the John Player League. His previous best analysis in this competition – 5-23 in 1969 – remained a county record for the next ten seasons. A virtual ever-present during his best years, he played all his first-class cricket apart from one match for the county, proving to be the most successful and valuable bowler for the county in some of its least successful seasons.

Paul John Franks
LHB & RFM, 1996-

Born: 3 February 1979, Sutton-in-Ashfield, Nottinghamshire

Batting

M	I	NO	Runs	HS
71	106	18	1983	85
91	62	25	706	60

Ave	50	100	ct/st
22.53	11	-	24
19.08	1	-	12

Bowling

Runs	Wkts	Av	BB	5wl	10wM
6613	235	28.14	7-56	8	-
3233	123	26.28	6-27	2	-

Best Performances
85 v. Middlesex, Lord's, 2001
60 v. Kent, Nottingham, 2002
7-56 v. Middlesex, Lord's, 2000
6-27 v. Durham, Chester-le-Street, 2000

Enjoying success from an early age, captaining England at both Under-15 and Under-17 levels, Paul Franks was soon involved in the first-class game at only seventeen years of age. In the final fixture of 1996, he experienced a tough baptism against Hampshire, whose 513/4 declared was their highest total against Nottinghamshire. In that context, figures of 2-65 off 28 overs represented a highly creditable performance. Thereafter his development as a first-class cricketer was rapid. Within two years, his quick medium-pace bowling had earned him a place at the head of the county's bowling averages, claiming most wickets and, at nineteen years of age, bowling the most overs. A year earlier he had become the youngest Nottinghamshire bowler to record a hat-trick, his achievement against Warwickshire coming at the age of 18 years and 163 days.

His career continued to blossom in 1999 when he was capped after taking 63 wickets in the Championship, performing equally well in one-day cricket, taking 5-27 against Glamorgan in the Sunday League and finishing with 22 wickets at the very economical cost of 16.22 apiece. His growing reputation was reflected in his continual selection for overseas tours, enhancing his claims to be an all-rounder in South Africa with the Under-19 side in 1997/98, when he captained the

side for a number of games and struck an unbeaten 119 in the second unofficial Test. He went on to be a member of the victorious England side in the Under-19 World Cup. Promoted to England A tours in both 1998/99 and 1999/2000 to Bangladesh and New Zealand, he proved to be the most successful bowler in the latter tour.

This success continued the following year when in the National League he surpassed his previous seasons' efforts with 25 wickets, including a career-best 6-27 against Durham. Coupled with a Championship career-best of 7-56 against Middlesex, he was rewarded with a place in the senior England NatWest squad against West Indies and Sri Lanka. With England already assured a place in the final, Franks was given a run-out on his home ground against the West Indies but experienced a very disappointing debut. Selection for a third England A tour followed, this time to the West Indies, but he was now to endure the first major setback in his career. After a good start to the 2001 season, which brought him a career-best 85 against Middlesex, a knee problem ended his cricket after only five games. Recovery has proved slow but sensibly he was not rushed back into action. Good performances in the Second XI brought him back into the county side where he was beginning to show his old form by the season's end, recognised by his initial selection on a provisional list of players for the Australian Academy. Still aged only twenty-four, and with a wealth of experience already behind him, he has both the talent and ambition to still go much further in the game.

Bruce Nicholas French ────────────────────────
RHB & WK, 1976-95

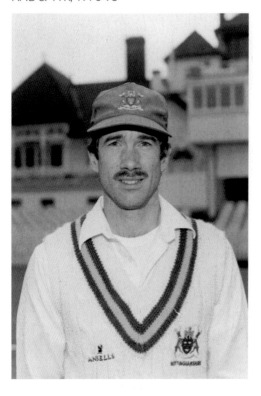

Born: 13 August 1959, Warsop, Nottinghamshire

Batting

M	I	NO	Runs	HS
324	427	83	6487	123
275	181	56	1896	49
Ave	50	100	ct/st	
18.85	22	2	737/ 92	
15.16	-	-	256/33	

Bowling

Runs	Wkts	Av	BB	5wI	10wM
70	1	70.00	1-37	-	-

Best Performances

123 v. Durham, Chester-le-Street, 1993
49 v. Staffordshire, Nottingham, 1985
1-37 v. Derbyshire, Derby, 1991

Bruce French was to become an integral part of a side which was to go on to claim two Championship titles and win all three limited-overs competitions. In addition he was to become the most capped Nottinghamshire wicketkeeper, appearing for England on sixteen occasions between 1986 and 1988. All the early signs suggested he was destined for the highest level in the game. A member of a successful North Nottinghamshire cricketing family, he made his first-class debut in 1976 against Cambridge University at the age of 16 years 287 days, the youngest player to appear for Notts in a first-class fixture. With Nottinghamshire lacking a specialist 'keeper, French became a regular member of the side in 1977, being voted Young Keeper of the Year. His Test potential was recognised the following year when he was selected for the England Under-19 team against the West Indies.

In the successful 1980s side, he proved to be one of the less noticeable members of a team brimming with volatile personalities. His brand of 'keeping was usually described as unobtrusive, neat, unhurried, polished, highly skilled and

efficient. This matched his consistent and quiet progress in the early stages of his county career, reflected in the number of dismissals per season, numbering over fifty in five consecutive seasons between 1981 and 1985. By 1984 his total of eighty-seven dismissals was not only a new county record but was the highest number by any 'keeper that season. It also included the new county record of ten dismissals in a match, achieved against Oxford University, beating his previous personal best of eight against Lancashire in 1981. Altogether he was to claim eight or more in a match on four occasions and six in an innings four times, both more than any other Notts 'keeper. Equally important, his batting improved in these years. He scored over 600 runs in three consecutive seasons from 1982 and 1984, whilst his highest score advanced to 98 in the latter year. More important was his best year of 1982, in which he scored 721 runs for the county, included 5 fifties, a sign of a consistent late middle-order batsman.

His involvement with the England side began in 1984/85, when he travelled to India as Downton's understudy, repeating the experience the following winter in the West Indies. He was finally capped in 1986, replacing Downton in the Second Test against India at Leeds and hold-

Bruce French – Nottinghamshire's most capped wicketkeeper.

ing his place for the remaining five Tests of the summer. This was despite a bizarre set of circumstances in the Lord's Test against New Zealand, when having been forced to retire hurt with concussion after a blow on the head from fellow Nottinghamshire player, Richard Hadlee, he returned to keep wicket for only the final ball in New Zealand's second innings, the fourth 'keeper to be tried in that innings. It was an incident which seemed to re-inforce the view that French was accident-prone, following on from being bitten by a dog whilst jogging in the West Indies and being struck on the head in the nets from a ball returned by a spectator in India in 1987/88.

An automatic selection as first 'keeper for the Ashes tour of 1986/87 under Mike Gatting, French was replaced by Richards, who was considered the better batsman. Restored to the England side in 1987, he appeared in eleven out of the next twelve Tests, with only a bout of chicken-pox interrupting this series of games against Pakistan and New Zealand. His highest Test innings, 59, against Pakistan at Old Trafford in 1987, was part of a fourth-wicket partnership of 113 with Tim Robinson. French, as with his 'keeping, always looked unhurried, comfortable and technically correct at the crease when batting, underlining the view that he was capable of scoring far more runs than he did. His undoubted skill and temperament were much in evidence in the NatWest Final of 1987 against Northamptonshire, when he arrived at the wicket with Notts still requiring 83 runs off the remaining 8.5 overs. His 35 off 27 deliveries in support of Richard Hadlee took Notts to the final over, the pair adding a vital 75 for the seventh wicket.

French's Test career was interrupted by a long-delayed operation to an injured finger in 1988, with further injuries in 1989 again putting him out of contention. His decision to join the rebel tour to South Africa at the end of that season effectively ended his Test career. He played four more full seasons for the county, 'keeping as well as ever with the third-highest number of dismissals in 1991, his benefit year. Ironically,

after being ruled out of Test cricket, he went on to score his only two first-class centuries, both being memorable efforts. His first, an unbeaten 105 against Derbyshire, was a highly courageous innings in an ill-tempered match between two Championship contenders; French saved the game against a hostile attack of Malcolm and Bishop, twice having to replace a damaged helmet. His 123 against Durham in 1993 was part of a seventh-wicket partnership of 301 with Chris Lewis, a county record.

French was to follow in the footsteps of previous Nottinghamshire wicketkeepers, such as Sherwin, Oates and Lilley, who all held the position of the county's wicketkeeper without challenge for many years. French was to retain the position for seventeen seasons until a viral infection affecting his eyes forced him into premature retirement in 1995. By this time he had accumulated the second-highest number of victims, 829, in the county's history, only Oates with 957 having taken more. However, his rate of 2.55 per match is superior to any other long-term Notts 'keeper.

Jason Edward Riche Gallian

RHB & RM, 1998-

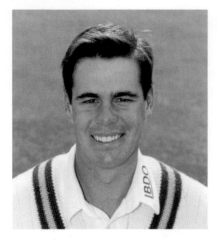

Born: 25 June 1971, Manly, Sydney, Australia

Batting

M	I	NO	Runs	HS
66	115	13	3482	171
79	77	4	2201	130
Ave	50	100	ct/st	
34.13	14	10	66	
30.15	13	2	26	

Bowling

Runs	Wkts	Av	BB	5wI	10wM
493	12	41.08	2-28	-	-
410	6	68.33	2-34	-	-

Best Performances

171 v. Glamorgan, Colwyn Bay, 2002
130 v. Derbyshire, Derby, 1999
2-28 v. Warwickshire, Nottingham, 1999
2-34 v. Yorkshire, Nottingham, 2000

When the Notts manager Alan Ormrod learnt that Gallian was unhappy with the terms offered by Lancashire, he was quick to sign on a player whom he had persuaded to join that county in 1990. Those four county seasons proved fruitful ones for the Australian opener, who achieved both a triple-century and an impressive county average of 42.41. It was a record which was to earn him three England caps and an Australian tour with England A in 1996/97.

His subsequent career at Nottinghamshire has proved a highly challenging one. Recovering from an early injury, and having just scored his maiden hundred for the county, carrying his bat for 113* against Hampshire, he took over the captaincy after Paul Johnson's resignation. He subsequently suffered a run of poor form, which saw him fail to reach fifty during the remainder of the season. By that time, Ormrod had also been dismissed, leaving Gallian to work with a new manager, Clive Rice. This unhappy start was not helped by a disastrous 1999 season, when ten defeats in the final eleven games resulted in the county under his leadership finishing in seventeenth place in the Championship. Yet Gallian's resilience has resulted in a continual improvement in his own performance and the county's fortunes.

By the close of the 2000 season, he was back at his best, scoring two consecutive centuries in the last three fixtures, both hard-hitting affairs, his 110* against Sussex taking only 115 balls and including 2 sixes and 17 fours. He also played a considerable part in the county's promotion in the National League by scoring 439 runs and participating in a record first-wicket stand of 196 with Bicknell. Sadly, he was to play only one game in 2001; a long drawn-out layoff after an operation being followed by a broken knuckle in his return in August.

He bounced back in 2002 to lead the county to promotion to Division One, enjoying his best season so far for Nottinghamshire. He scored over 1,000 runs at an average of over forty, experiencing a highly consistent season which included 4 hundreds and 6 fifties. He played a significant part in two victories, scoring an unbeaten 111* against Northamptonshire, he and Afzaal sharing an unbroken third-wicket partnership of 183 to secure a seven-wicket win. The second occasion, another unbeaten hundred, this time against promotion rival Derbyshire, was a major turning point in the county's fortunes. Requiring 323 for victory, he batted throughout the innings to partner Greg Smith in a tenth-wicket partnership of 46 to claim an unexpected one-wicket victory, beginning a sequence of victories which eventually won promotion. Now an established Nottinghamshire player, who has already made more appearances for his new county than for Lancashire, Gallian's understated captaincy and calm, consistent batting could well make an important contribution to the county's success in Division One in 2003.

Gamini Goonesena
RHB & LB, 1952-64

Born: 16 February 1931, Colombo, Ceylon

Batting

M	I	NO	Runs	HS
94	146	17	2464	107*
Ave	50	100	ct/st	
19.10	9	1	52	

Bowling

Runs	Wkts	Av	BB	5wI	10wM
7495	299	25.06	7-63	19	3

Best Performances
107* v. Northamptonshire, Nottingham, 1955
7-63 v. Leicestershire, Leicester, 1958

A diminutive leg-break bowler and a more than useful middle-order batsman, Goonesena, although reserving his best performances for other sides, still proved a valuable member of the team, which enjoyed a brief renaissance during his time with the county. Having played for Ceylon at the age of sixteen, he was offered a three-year contract whilst in England in 1952. Having served out his one-year residential qualification, he had the good fortune to come into an attack bolstered by the arrival of the Australian Test player, Bruce Dooland. Their first match in tandem provided a timely reminder that wickets would not come easily on the placid Trent Bridge pitch, their combined analysis in Kent's first innings being one wicket for 218 runs! Relief about the two new signings soon came when, against the Champions Surrey in the Whit Bank holiday fixture, the pair shared all ten wickets in the visitors' first innings.

Unfortunately for the county, Goonesena went up to Cambridge in 1954, giving up his professional status to become an amateur, and was able to play for the county in only the second part of the season for four years. Even so, his support for Dooland proved useful, and for a leg-spinner his wickets were taken at an economical cost, his highest average between 1954 and 1957 being 22.53. His best season for the county was in 1955 when, after an excellent season for Cambridge, he went on to become the first player to complete the double in that year; when needing both runs and wickets, he scored 61

runs and took seven wickets against Kent and was awarded his county cap. He ended the season with 57 Championship wickets out of his season's total of 134, finishing ahead of Dooland in the county's averages. He was also making runs, having moved up the order, scoring his maiden Championship hundred in the final home match of the season.

He again enjoyed an excellent season in 1957, once again completing the double. His major successes that year were with the university, when as captain he scored 211 in the Varsity match. He returned to Notts in fine form, taking 7-75 against Derbyshire in his first game and again completed the double in fine style when he made a half-century and took nine wickets against Leicestershire. With Dooland's departure at the end of the 1957 season, it was hoped that Goonesena would compensate for his loss but although appearing in more games for the county than in any other season, both his batting and bowling form proved inconsistent. Against Leicestershire, however, he did manage to record both his best innings, 7-63, and match figures, 13-82, for the county. He left the county at the end of the season and after a spell with New South Wales returned to England in 1964, appearing for Notts in the closing weeks of the season. He made an immediate impression with five wickets in his first outing in seven years, repeating this achievement in his penultimate Championship game. It was a pointed reminder of how the county could have done with his all-round contributions during those missing years.

James Grundy

RHB & RF (round-arm), 1851-67

Born: 5 March 1824, New Radford, Nottingham
Died: 24 November 1873, Carrington, Nottingham

Batting

M	I	NO	Runs	HS
53	86	7	981	76*
Ave	50	100	ct/st	
2.41	3	-	41	

Bowling

Runs	Wkts	Av	BB	5wI	10wM
2168	175(7)	12.45	9-19	12	-

Best Performances
76* v. Cambridgeshire, Cambridge, 1862
9-19 v. Kent, Nottingham, 1864

Although James Grundy's career didn't take off until 1851 at the age of twenty-seven, he was to become one of the most sought after all-rounders in the country. In his first full season he was to make debuts for Nottinghamshire, the MCC, the Players, the North and Clarke's All-England XI, taking 114 wickets, the most by any bowler in England. It marked the first occasion a bowler had taken 100 wickets in his first full season, Grundy having appeared previously in only one first-class fixture. The following year, he again took over 100 wickets. These were the only two seasons he was to achieve this target.

For Nottinghamshire, he was to appear in fifty-two out of fifty-three possible matches between 1851 and 1867, missing one game in his final season when he stood as an umpire after forty-eight consecutive appearances. He was to prove a fine all-round player, often opening the batting and occupying every position in the batting order for the county in his sixteen years' service. He also achieved success as a round-arm fast-medium bowler, being especially noted for his accuracy. Mynn's *In Memorium* included the lines, 'Jimmy Grundy's cool and clever, almost always on the spot.' He once bowled 84 balls to Parr and Daft without conceding a run.

After making his debut against Surrey in 1851, the first-ever meeting between the two counties, he followed this with match figures of 10-86 against Surrey at Trent Bridge the following year. He was twice more to take ten wickets in a match against Surrey. His best match figures for Nottinghamshire were against Sussex, his 10-43 including a remarkable analysis of 5-6 in the second innings. He took 9-19 against Kent in 1864, still the best innings figures returned by a Nottinghamshire bowler at Trent Bridge and the county's best analysis until 1956. He had a reputation for saving lost causes, his most noteworthy bowling in this respect being against Yorkshire in 1863 at Trent Bridge. The visitors, requiring 101 for victory, were thwarted by Grundy's 5-13, Notts winning by six runs. Grundy was carried shoulder-high to the pavilion and received a collection of £15. In 1864, he almost snatched victory from a Surrey side requiring 62 for victory and being 40-1 when Grundy took five wickets for no runs, Surrey eventually scrambling home by one wicket. He had his moments with the bat, making three scores of over fifty, his best being 76 against Cambridgeshire in 1862.

When he retired in 1869 he had appeared in 298 important fixtures, the second-highest number by any cricketer, having scored the fourth-highest number of runs (5,898), taken the fourth-highest number of wickets (1,137), and taken the most catches (233).

George Gunn
RHB & RS, 1902-32

Born: 13 June 1879, Hucknall Torkard, Nottinghamshire
Died: 29 June 1958, Cuckfield, Sussex

Batting

M	I	NO	Runs	HS
583	959	74	31592	220
Ave	**50**	**100**	**ct/st**	
35.69	176	55	428	

Bowling

Runs	Wkts	Av	BB	5wI	10wM
2183	61	35.78	5-50	1	-

Best Performances

220 v. Derbyshire, Nottingham, 1923
5-50 v. Middlesex, Nottingham, 1905

'One of the cricketing marvels of the age. No man has ever made batting look so simple.' This reference in *Wisden* in 1928 came when Gunn, aged forty-nine, was enjoying one of his most productive seasons, recording his highest aggregate for the county, 1886 runs, and overtaking Arthur Shrewsbury's total of centuries for Nottinghamshire. Among his 6 centuries that year was a sublime hundred against Kent at Trent Bridge, taking only 95 minutes; *Wisden* noted that he 'seized on the occasion for a demonstration of his exceptional batting skill'. Even this was not George's swansong. One year later, an ever-present, he became, along with Payton, the member of a Championship-winning side for the second time, the last occasion having been twenty-two years earlier. Both times he had made a significant contribution. In 1907 he topped the county's batting averages; in 1929 he scored 1,788 runs and 4 hundreds, including a century on his fiftieth birthday. Two years later, at the age of fifty-two, he became the oldest batsman to score a century for Nottinghamshire, as well as passing 1,000 runs in a season for the twentieth time, another county record. The most pleasurable moment in that year must have come against Warwickshire, when both he and his son, George Vernon, scored a century in the same innings, a unique achievement. When his career came to a close the following year, shortened by being struck by a head-high fast full toss, he had scored more runs and most centuries for the county as well as making the most appearances.

However, it was not these statistics which drove so many cricket writers to put pen to paper about George Gunn. From Neville Cardus (George was a particular favourite of his) to E.W. Swanton, all were fascinated by him. Here was a batsman of exceptional talent and skill, possessing high technical ability, a player of the highest class, recognised as one of the finest players of fast bowling, with that true mark of the really great batsman – the ability to play his shots with time to spare. What confounded them all was his approach to the game: he was a batsman who, for no obvious reason, deliberately stonewalled mediocre bowling and unleashed the most brilliant and audacious shots against top-class attacks. Stories abound about his giving his wicket away because 'it was too hot' or because he always had lunch at 1.30 p.m. and was not prepared to bat on until 2.00 p.m. His fielding was also idiosyncratic, Arthur Carr asserting that George, an exceptionally fine slip fielder, always liked if possible to catch the ball one-handed. In the West Indies, he is said to have stood underneath a steepling catch in the deep with his hat outstretched in his hand, only to catch the ball with the other.

George Gunn's fiftieth birthday 1929. Mr A.W. Carr presenting gifts from himself and the players.

He was, however, never inconsistent for he only failed to reach 1,000 runs three times between 1905 and 1931. He made only one double-century but passed 150 on ten other occasions. By 1910 he was opening the innings, with Whysall participating in 40 hundred partnerships. Gunn's tenacity as an opening batsman is recognised by his record of carrying his bat for the county on eight occasions. Three times he scored a hundred in each innings of a match, against Surrey at Trent Bridge in 1919, his aggregate of 354 in the match being the highest number scored by a Notts batsman in one game. His 132 and 109* against Yorkshire illustrates the oft-quoted reference about his approach to batting: 'I always bats according.' In this match after batting for six hours and being riled by the Yorkshire bowlers for his slowness, he then proceeded to strike an unbeaten 109 out of 129 in 90 minutes. A similar incident occurred on his Test debut when allegedly annoyed by a suggestion from a team member about his ability, he responded with 119 and 74, becoming the fifth England batsman to make a century on debut. In a different mood, he fulfilled a promise to Cardus that he would make a hundred on his fiftieth birthday.

He was to appear in only one Test in England, although enjoying two successful tours to Australia. Not in the original 1907/08 party but convalescing after a lung disorder, he headed both tour and Test averages. In 1911/12 he again averaged over forty in Tests and over fifty in all matches. Above all, his omission from the England side in 1921 still remains a complete mystery. With England needing a batsman to stand up to the combined pace attack of Gregory and McDonald, thirty players were called up, but Gunn was not among them. John Arlott was later to comment that 'there was never a more tragic waste of great ability and character'. Incredibly, Gunn was selected for England for one more series, recalled at the age of fifty after an interval of over seventeen years to tour the West Indies, averaging 34.50 in the Tests.

After retirement he ran his own cricket side, was a member of the Nottinghamshire committee and was a regular visitor to Trent Bridge. He remains one of the county's most loved characters and certainly one of the most gifted.

George Vernon Gunn
RHB & LB, 1928-50

Born: 21 July 1905, West Bridgford, Nottingham
Died: 15 October 1957, Shelton, Shrewsbury

Batting

M	I	NO	Runs	HS
264	391	43	10225	184
Ave	50	100	ct/st	
29.38	56	11	114	

Bowling

Runs	Wkts	Av	BB	5wI	10wM
10026	281	35.67	7-44	9	1

Best Performances
184 v. Leicestershire, Nottingham, 1938
7-44 v. Essex, Nottingham, 1932

G.V. Gunn was one of a number of promising young batsmen who waited patiently for the opportunity to break into the successful, elderly, settled Nottinghamshire side of the late 1920s. Eventually, Keeton, Harris, Hardstaff and Gunn himself were to become established members of the county side, with all but Gunn surviving to play after the Second World War. The son of the exceptionally talented George Gunn and the fourth member of the Gunn family to play for the county, G.V.'s career proved to be the least exceptional of the four.

From 1925 to 1930, he served his apprenticeship in the Second XI, topping the batting averages in the final two years and, after making his debut in 1928, played in seven Championship games in 1929, making an impressive 73 in the game marking his father's fiftieth birthday presentation. The break-up of the twenties side in 1931 gave him the opportunity to appear in fifteen games, the high watermark for 'Young George' being his maiden first-class century against Warwickshire in the same innings in which his father also reached three figures, the only occurrence in the first-class game. The following season he began to be thought of as a possible all-round prospect when he took 7-44 against Essex at Trent Bridge. This promise was underlined in 1934 when his 826 runs were supplemented by 72 wickets, including match figures of 10-120 against Hampshire, which contributed to a narrow 8-run victory.

An ability to bowl both off- and leg-breaks with the occasional googly appeared to make him a replacement for the veteran Sam Staples. However, his first 1,000 runs in a season in 1935, which included two fine attacking hundreds, was counter-balanced by a deterioration in his bowling, which became increasingly costly. He went on to score over 1,000 runs in the next four seasons. His best year came in 1937 when he averaged over forty for the only time in his career, scoring a total of 1,763 in all games. The following year saw his highest innings for the county, 184 against Leicestershire, one of 11 hundreds for Nottinghamshire. The Second World War ended his first-class career, G.V. opting to remain in League cricket after the war. He was, however, to make one final appearance for the county when he was recalled in an injury crisis against Derbyshire in 1950, aged forty-five, but sadly he lasted only two deliveries. He was to die in a motorcycle accident in 1957, less than a year before the death of his father.

G.V. was a decent county cricketer: an attractive middle-order batsman, who occasionally deputised as an opening batsman. It was his lot to be the son of a unique cricketer and to be seen by some as another great prospect. Given the impossibility of being another George Gunn, he still remained a cheerful, optimistic and enthusiastic player with a love for the game.

John Richmond Gunn
LHB & LM/SLA, 1896-1925

Born: 19 July 1876, Hucknall Torkard, Nottinghamshire

Died: 21 August 1963, Basford, Nottingham

Batting

M	I	NO	Runs	HS
489	769	94	23194	294
Ave	50	100	ct/st	
34.36	119	40	215	

Bowling

Runs	Wkts	Av	BB	5wI	10wM
27339	1128	24.23	8-63	75	16

Best Performances
294 v. Leicestershire, Nottingham, 1903
8-63 v. Surrey, The Oval, 1903

Statistically, John Gunn is the greatest all-rounder ever to play for the county. He is the only player to score over 20,000 runs and to take over 1,000 wickets. He stands as the fourth-highest run-scorer and the eighth-highest wicket-taker. He completed the double in four consecutive seasons between 1903 and 1906; three of them in county matches alone, a feat that no other Nottinghamshire player can match. In addition, he was recognised as an outstanding specialist cover point, possessing an accurate, fast throw.

Following his debut in 1896, aged twenty-one, his all-round qualities soon emerged in the following season when in consecutive games he scored his maiden first-class hundred against the touring Philadelphians and match figures of 10-136 against Yorkshire. Beginning as a medium-pacer, over the years he reduced his pace, ending as a slow left-arm bowler by 1906. In 1903 he took 100 wickets for the first time, heading the county's bowling averages. He returned career-best innings and match figures of 8-63 and 14-132 against Surrey at The Oval, part of a purple patch in which he claimed forty-three wickets in seven consecutive innings. His 110 wickets in 1906, his third and last 100 wickets in a season, was his most productive for the county. By this time he had recorded his two hat-tricks: his first against Middlesex in 1899 and, his second against Derbyshire in 1904, coming from his first three balls in their second innings.

His batting was of a consistently good standard. He headed the batting averages in 1912, 1914 and 1920, scoring 40 centuries and reaching 1,000 runs on eleven occasions Twice he was to score over a hundred runs in a pre-lunch session, the second time in probably his greatest all-round match. At Trent Bridge against Gloucestershire in 1911, he scored 94 and an unbeaten 150, moving from 26* to 150* in the morning session, as well as taking 6-60. He was to repeat the feat of a century and ten wickets in a match in 1921 against Lancashire, the only Nottinghamshire player to achieve this on two occasions. He also scored over a hundred runs in a pre-lunch session in his 294 in 1903, the only double-century of his career and his first Championship three-figure innings, at that time the highest innings by a Notts batsman.

In the closing years of his career, he became increasingly overweight, only left out of the side for the first time in 1925, his final season. Aged forty-nine, he enjoyed one last moment of glory, scoring 166 when recalled at the last minute to play against Hampshire at Southampton.

He continued to appear for Julien Cahn's XI until the age of fifty-five. He played six times for England, appearing in all five Tests in the 1901/02 tour of Australia and against Australia at Trent Bridge in 1905. After his playing days were over he retained his enthusiasm for the game, becoming with his brother, George, a regular spectator at Trent Bridge.

William Gunn

RHB & RS (round-arm), 1880-1904

Born: 4 December 1858, St Anne's, Nottingham
Died: 29 January 1921, Nottingham

Batting

M	I	NO	Runs	HS
363	585	48	18295	273
Ave	50	100	ct/st	
34.06	93	34	237/1	

Bowling

Runs	Wkts	Av	BB	5wI	10wM
1196	41	29.17	4-27	-	-

Best Performances
Batting: 273 v. Derbyshire, Derby, 1901
Bowling: 4-27 v. Leicestershire, Leicester, 1894

If Arthur Shrewsbury was the dominant batsman in Nottinghamshire cricket in the 1880s and 1890s, Billy Gunn proved an exceptionally close second. Physically quite different – Gunn at 6ft 3in, standing 7in higher than his county colleague and much more powerfully built – they represented what became known as the Nottingham school of batting. The Nottingham Giant, as he was often described, made full use of his long reach and commanding height but he was essentially a member of the classical school. With a very upright stance and an absolutely straight bat, he excelled in the cover drive. He was not a hitter and very rarely hooked or pulled, his main concern being to keep the ball down, for as he once explained, 'I can make as big hits as anyone I like but if I begin to lift the ball, I never score more than forty.' Constantly described as elegant, graceful and a model of classical orthodoxy, he was also, like Shrewsbury, an innings-builder, proceeding patiently at a uniform pace towards a large total. Like Shrewsbury, he adopted the technique of pad play, both being criticised for the slowness of their batting. As one contemporary cricketer remarked, 'Gunn and Shrewsbury began playing for a draw at 12.00 on the first day.' Many bowlers must have agreed as the pair were involved in 26 century partnerships, 7 of them over 200. The Sussex bowlers particularly suffered, as the pair added 398 for the second wicket in 1890 and 312 for the same wicket in 1891.

Gunn made his debut in 1880 after impressing in local cricket and being chosen for the Colts of England against MCC. It was the manner in which he made his runs that attracted comment, *The Times* observing that 'when he first appeared at Lord's his style was so good that there were several old cricketers who foretold a big future for him.' Gunn benefited from being the member of a very successful Nottinghamshire side in the mid-1880s and was able to cement a permanent place in the eleven during the professionals' strike of 1881, when seven of the current established members refused the county's terms. It was in his fifth season, aged twenty-six, that his early promise began to bear fruit. He scored his maiden hundred and enjoyed his first big partnership with Shrewsbury, 266 for the fifth wicket against Sussex, a world record. A year later, he recorded his first double-century when appearing for MCC against Yorkshire, featuring in another world-record partnership, 330 for the fourth wicket with fellow county player Billy Barnes. His predilection for huge partnerships surfaced again in 1903 when he added 369 for the third wicket with his nephew, John Gunn, yet another world first-class record.

The year 1885 had established his reputation as one of the leading professional batsmen of his day, and in 1889 he stood at the head of the national batting averages, doing so again in 1893. It was the most productive year of his career, Gunn scoring over 1,000 runs for the

John, William and George Gunn, all great servants of the Nottinghamshire club.

William Gunn

John. Gunn.

George Gunn

virtual automatic choice at home between 1888 and 1896, he took part in only one overseas tour, being more concerned to remain in England to oversee his business interests. He played one outstanding innings against the Australian tourists in 1890 for the Players of England, his 228 in 9 ¾ hours being the highest innings played against the visitors in England. His only Test hundred came in 1893; his 102 at Old Trafford was the first Test century at that ground. Fittingly, he appeared for England for the last time in 1899 at Trent Bridge in the first ever Test to be played at that ground.

Gunn was also an accomplished soccer player, playing the majority of his games for Notts County from 1881 to 1893, scoring 64 goals in 144 appearances as a skilful, speedy outside-left. He was selected for England to play in two internationals in 1884. He subsequently became a director of the club and after the close of his first-class cricket career was also to join the Nottinghamshire committee. By this time he was a wealthy local businessman, the co-founder of the Gunn & Moore sports goods firm, established in 1885. He died in 1921, aged sixty-three and a very wealthy man, leaving an estate of £60,000; he was one of a number of successful professional cricketers who had made their fortune from the game. A great professional batsman of his era, he was also one of the most pleasing to watch. William Oscroft, who stood down from the county side in 1882 against the visiting Australians to allow Gunn to play, best summed it up when he remarked that he 'would rather watch Gunn make fifty than W.G. or Arthur Shrewsbury make a hundred'.

county, the second to do so after Shrewsbury, and over 2,000 in all matches, hitting 7 hundreds. In all, Gunn made 1,000 runs in a season on twelve occasions but his value to the county was seen in his 1,000 runs in the five seasons from 1893 to 1903. Five of his eight double-centuries came in this latter part of his career, including a career-best 273 against Derbyshire in 1901 at the age of forty-two. These innings were constantly described as flawless, chanceless, without blemish or 'as near perfection as it would be possible to attain'.

He was never able to carry this form consistently into the Test arena, his eleven appearances yielding a modest average of 21.77. A

Born: 30 July 1813, Nottingham
Died: 15 April 1873, Nottingham

Batting

M	I	NO	Runs	HS
28	48	2	619	73*
Ave	50	100	ct/st	
13.45	2	-	25/8	

Best Performances
73* v. Kent, Town Malling, 1840

Joseph Guy (far left of picture) was a local cricketer who became one of the first Nottinghamshire batsmen to make an impression outside his native county, playing regularly at the highest level for most of his cricketing career. An unassuming individual, he lacked the extrovert nature of other Nottinghamshire players of this era, such as William Clarke and George Parr, but was still regarded as one of the best batsmen in England. He was the first Nottinghamshire batsman to play on a regular basis at Lord's in all the principal fixtures of the day.

He was a batsman of the traditional and conservative school, often referred to as a scientific batsman, who remained wedded to the old methods of keeping in his crease and playing any straight ball back to the bowler. He was noted for his elegant style, often described in his era as second only to Fuller Pitch in that respect. William Clarke in an oft-quoted observation stated, 'Joe Guy; all ease and elegance, fit to play before her Majesty in a drawing room.' He kept wicket on many occasions and was an excellent longstop, a vital position in his era. Excelling in forward defence, he was at times a slow scorer: against Twenty of Leicester in 1849, he occupied the crease for five hours on the first day and four on the second in accumulating 55 runs. He was sometimes accused of sacrificing run-getting to show off his stylish defence.

At the age of twenty-three, he made a highly promising county debut against Sussex in 1837, whose attack included Lillywhite; his second innings score of 21 out of a total of 64 making him the only batsman to reach double figures. Top-scoring in the two remaining fixtures of the season, such a good start promised a highly successful future. He appeared in 30 of the 32 games for which he was available in his eighteen seasons with the county. For a time he held the county record for the highest individual innings, an unbeaten 73* against Kent in 1840 at Town Malling, beating William Clarke's 65 against Sheffield in 1834. It contributed to a ten-wicket victory, the county's highest win so far in an important match. His other innings of over fifty for Nottinghamshire came against Surrey at The Oval in 1852, the county winning by an innings and 52 runs, Notts' biggest victory in an inter-county fixture.

During his career he was a virtual automatic selection for all the major representative games, appearing in 55 out of the 57 major fixtures at Lord's for which he was eligible between 1828 and 1852. He was also a regular player for Clarke's All-England XI, participating in the first fixture in 1846 and going on to appear in 175 games.

Richard John Hadlee

LHB & RF, 1978-87

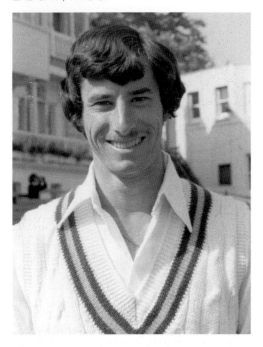

Born: 3 July 1951, St Albans, Christchurch, New Zealand

Batting

M	I	NO	Runs	HS
148	196	45	5854	210*
159	136	33	2951	100*
Ave	50	100	ct/st	
38.76	29	11	105	
28.65	11	1	58	

Bowling

Runs	Wkts	Av	BB	5wI	10wM
9031	622	14.51	8-41	38	5
4156	231	17.99	6-12	3	-

Best Performances

210* v. Middlesex, Lord's, 1984
100 v. Gloucestershire, Cheltenham, 1982*
8-41 v. Lancashire, Nottingham, 1985
6-12 v. Lancashire, Nottingham, 1980

John Woodcock, listing Richard Hadlee at 29th in his *One Hundred Greatest Cricketers*, wrote that 'he was feared more when he was thirty-five than when he had been twenty-five, which is very rare for a fast bowler'. It was Nottinghamshire's good fortune that during his ten seasons he matured from a very good fast bowler into a world-class all-rounder, bringing in his wake two Championship titles and a first-ever limited-overs trophy. Equally it was Hadlee's experience of county cricket which brought about a fundamental change in his approach to bowling; one New Zealand writer commented that his 'involvement in county cricket produced the life-saving element of his career'. Hadlee's involvement with Nottinghamshire was fortuitous, brought about by the temporary sacking of Clive Rice in 1976. The county, needing to find a rapid replacement, offered Hadlee, in England at the time, a three-year contract.

Hadlee joined Nottinghamshire soon after making his mark in Test cricket, his match figures of 10-100 sending England to their first-ever defeat against New Zealand in 1978. He was still at this stage of his career a typical young fast bowler, relying essentially on pace and belligerence, as well as being a useful and aggressive lower-order hitter. He was to appear in a mere twenty-three Championship games in his initial three-year contract, the consequence of commitments to the New Zealand side in 1978 and then, more worryingly, a number of injuries in the following seasons. He began impressively, in his first five Championship appearances claiming 34 wickets, including 11-141 against Yorkshire, also striking his maiden first-class hundred – a hard-hitting 101*, containing 3 sixes and 13 fours against Derbyshire in 150 minutes. He also finished on a high note in 1980 with 6-12 in his final Sunday League game, a new county record. In all three years, he headed the county's bowling averages.

Hadlee, worried by injuries brought about by continuous cricket and upset by his failure to appear in sufficient games to honour his contract, was reluctant to continue his county career, eventually being persuaded to remain with the county on a yearly basis. This decision prompted a reappraisal of his bowling approach, involving a reduced run-up. This in turn was to produce far greater accuracy and led to the development of new techniques, including a concentration on seam and swing, with his away swinger becoming a lethal ball. This coupled with dedicated work at his fitness levels paid off, both for him and the county. Appearing in every Championship game,

Richard Hadlee, a vital ingredient in the county's two Championship successes of the 1980s.

plus nineteen limited-over fixtures, he was the only bowler in the country to reach a hundred wickets, again heading the national bowling averages. His batting too played its part in the county's Championship success. In addition to a career-best 142* against Yorkshire, he played a vital innings against second-placed Surrey in August, when an aggressive 98 in 129 minutes enabled Notts to win the game inside two days.

Hadlee remained with the county for the next six seasons, playing in the majority of Championship games, apart from 1983 and 1986 when international commitments limited his appearances. It is significant that in 1983, when Hadlee made only five appearances, the county experienced its worst year since he joined them, slipping to fourteenth in the table. His contribution in these years was magnificent, for in all six seasons he headed the county's bowling averages and three times the national averages, coming second on two other occasions. In 1984 he became the first player since 1967 to complete the double, and only the fourth Nottinghamshire player, the last having been Bruce Dooland in 1957. It was achieved by a meticulously-planned set of pre-season objectives, an example of single-minded determination. He worked equally hard on his batting technique, which was reflected in his career-best undefeated 210* against Middlesex at Lord's. Coming in at 17-4 he reached his hundred in 93 balls, but then changed the whole pace of his innings to ensure a large first-innings total to secure an innings victory. He also proved an all-round match winner against Hampshire, coming in at 134-5 facing a total of 303 and hitting an unbeaten 100 to gain first-innings points, following up with 5-35, Notts scraping home by two wickets.

In 1985 he recorded his best figures for the county, 8-41 against Lancashire, but it was his final season in 1987 when he achieved his greatest success, heading both the county's batting and bowling averages with figures of 53.75 and 11.89 respectively, the latter his best bowling average for Notts. It was a season filled with personal highlights: a hat-trick against Kent, the match double of a century and twelve wickets against Somerset, as well as a critical contribution in the closing fixtures of the season, when he followed his 10-46 against Sussex with 6-38 in the final innings of the season against Glamorgan. He was just three wickets short of completing another memorable double. He was largely responsible for Nottinghamshire's first-ever limited-overs trophy. Requiring 145 in 21 overs with only five wickets standing, Hadlee hit an unbeaten 70 in 61 balls, striking a six and four off successive deliveries in the final over of the game to secure the NatWest Trophy.

Hadlee's record firmly establishes him as one of the county's greatest all-rounders. Of the twelve Nottinghamshire cricketers who have scored over 5,000 runs and taken over 500 wickets, he possesses the highest batting and the lowest bowling average. He was the essential additional element in a talented side, which was to make the 1980s a decade of high achievement for the county.

Born: 12 November 1869, East Leake, Nottinghamshire
Died: 24 July 1940, Loughborough, Leicestershire

Batting

M	I	NO	Runs	HS
194	261	73	1986	57
Ave	50	100	ct/st	
10.56	2	-	112	

Bowling

Balls	Runs	Wkts	Av	5wI	10wM
14565	767	18.98	8-67	51	10

Best Performances
57 v. Lancashire, Manchester, 1908
8-67 v. Middlesex, Lord's, 1907

'There seems little or no chance that he will ever be able to bear the strain of county matches again,' was *Wisden*'s verdict on Hallam at the close of the 1899 season. Two seasons earlier the Lancashire bowler had taken a hundred wickets in all matches. Struck by illness but believed to have recovered, he made a return appearance, only to collapse in mid-over. A few more games did follow, but with little success.

It was Arthur Shrewsbury whose recommendation earned him a fresh start, for Hallam was qualified by birth to play for Nottinghamshire. He made a sensational start in the pre-season fixture between the First XI and XXII Colts, taking 17-48 in their second innings, twelve being clean-bowled. After a remarkable first season in 1901, when he headed the Notts averages with 64 wickets, the following four seasons were undramatic. Then, aged thirty-six, he was to experience two outstanding years, the second culminating in Nottinghamshire becoming Champions in 1907, Hallam thus enjoying the distinction of having appeared in a Championship side for two counties. A year earlier he had achieved sixth place in the national averages, taking 104 wickets, and was rated as one of the best medium-pace bowlers in the country and often likened to William Attewell, renowned for his unerring accuracy.

The wet season of 1907 was to provide extremely suitable pitches for Hallam's type of bowling and also for his partner, Nottingham-shire's most prolific bowler, Tom Wass. The pair ran through practically every side in the Championship, twice bowling unchanged in a match and eight times in an innings. Hallam finished top of the national averages with 168 wickets at 12.69 apiece, 156 for Notts, the highest number by a bowler for the county, had it not been for Wass claiming 163 in the same season. Hallam claimed a hat-trick against Leicestershire and also returned his best innings figures for Notts: 8-67 against Middlesex at Lord's, the second and last time he was to take eight in an innings for the county. This was a match-winning performance, as an unbeaten Middlesex, requiring 153 for victory, were 44-0 before Hallam bowled 'in deadly form'. His best match figures, 13-56 against Essex, also came in this season. He was named as one of *Wisden*'s Five Cricketers of the Year and was considered unfortunate not to have appeared against the visiting South Africans. He had been invited to appear in the Third Test but had to decline on account of a badly bruised hand.

He was never to get another chance for his country. Although just missing 100 wickets in all matches in 1908, he was handicapped by rheumatism in the right shoulder and, appearing in only four games in 1910, decided to return to the Lancashire League. There he returned some staggering analyses for Nelson in 1911 and 1912, once taking seven wickets in nine balls and claiming all ten in another fixture.

Joe Hardstaff (Snr)
RHB & RFM, 1902-24

Born: 9 November 1882, Kirkby-in-Ashfield,
   Nottinghamshire
Died: 2 April 1947, Nuncargate, Nottinghamshire

Batting

M	I	NO	Runs	HS
340	560	70	15059	213*
Ave	**50**	**100**	**ct/st**	
30.73	81	22	171/2	

Bowling

Runs	Wkts	Av	BB	5wI	10wM
2124	55	38.61	5-133	1	-

Best Performances
213* v. Sussex, Hove, 1914
5-133 v. Australians, Nottingham, 1921

One of the smallest players to appear for the county, Joe Hardstaff at only 5ft 6in enjoyed a highly successful career with Nottinghamshire before going on to become one of the game's most respected umpires. He stood in 21 Tests, eventually having to retire when his son began his Test career in 1935. A sturdy, stocky man, whose boyish features in his early career caused him to be barred from entering Lord's by the gateman on the grounds that he was both too young and too small to be a player, he proved to be a highly entertaining and aggressive middle-order batsman and a brilliant fielder in the deep. Essentially a fast scorer, he was capable of scoring all round the wicket and was especially strong on the square cut and the pull.

His undoubted natural ability earned him a place on the ground staff in 1902 at the age of nineteen, although it was not until 1904 that he claimed a regular place in the side. Playing in a strong batting side, his progress was steady rather than spectacular, the county being willing to persevere with a player of such apparent natural ability, of whom great things were expected. His maiden century came in 1905 and the following year, 1906, he passed 1,000 runs in all matches for the first time. A chance-less century for the Players at The Oval, his first representative appearance, created a very favourable impression. This was reinforced the following year, when not only was he a productive and ever-present member of a Championship-winning side,

but he also scored 124*, all before lunch on the second day against the visiting South Africans, one of only four hundreds hit against the tourists. It won him a place in the touring party to visit Australia in 1907/08, a tour that was to prove the highlight of his cricketing career. He played in all five Tests, averaging 31.10, and was the only player to make over 1,000 runs, at an average of 52.30. His aggressive approach won him many friends in Australia, earning him the nickname of 'Hotstuff'.

Hardstaff headed the Notts averages in 1908, scoring 1,000 runs for the county for the first time, but unfortunately for him England played no further Tests until 1909, when he failed to win a place against Australia, never again being selected for an England side. He continued to be one of the county's best batsmen for the remainder of his career, scoring 1,000 runs for the county on six occasions; his best year being 1911, when, scoring 5 hundreds, he amassed 1,482 runs at an average of 46.31. In the same year, he became the third Notts batsman to score a century in both innings of a match, making 118 and 106* against Derbyshire at Trent Bridge. The only double-century of his career came in 1914, against Sussex at Hove, when he scored an unbeaten 213*. He claimed five wickets in an innings on only one occasion, his 5-133 occurring in the county's greatest defeat by an innings and 517 runs against the Australians in 1921.

Born: 3 July 1911, Nuncargate, Nottinghamshire
Died: 1 January 1990, Worksop, Nottinghamshire

Batting

M	I	NO	Runs	HS
408	632	73	24249	266
Ave	50	100	ct/st	
43.37	123	65	89	

Bowling

Runs	Wkts	Av	BB	5wl	10wM
1635	28	58.39	4-43	-	-

Best Performances

266 v. Leicestershire, Leicester, 1937
4-43 v. Lancashire, Manchester, 1947

One of the better known cricket photographs shows a smiling Joe Hardstaff, standing alongside Don Bradman, about to congratulate Len Hutton on achieving the highest individual score in Test cricket. Hardstaff went on to make an unbeaten 169, his highest innings against Australia, after sharing a record sixth-wicket partnership of 215 against Australia with Hutton in this Oval Test of 1938, which saw England establish a new Test record of 903-7 declared. An automatic choice in the England side, war was to rob him at his peak of six years of first-class cricket. Although he was to appear in a further seven Tests in the post-war years, he never again commanded the position he had held in 1939.

'Young Joe', as he was often referred to, was the son of Test cricketer and umpire Joe Hardstaff. Recommended by Larwood, Hardstaff admitted he would have played for Nottinghamshire for next to nothing at the time. Scoring an unbeaten 53 in his first first-class innings in 1930 and an unbeaten hundred in only his fourth first-class appearance at the age of nineteen, he did not secure a regular place in the side until 1934. He, along with Keeton, Harris and G.V. Gunn, competed for places in an experienced and settled Nottinghamshire side, but by 1934 he had moved up to number three in the batting order, playing in every Championship game, and scoring 4 hundreds in a total aggre-

gate of 1,817 runs at an average of just over forty.

It was not just the runs scored or his brilliance in the outfield, which began to attract attention; it was the manner in which the runs were made. Possessing a beautifully upright and settled stance, his high backlift and quick footwork allowed him to play all the orthodox strokes, his speciality being the cover drive. A classic batsman, Jim Swanton remarked that 'he would have adorned any team in any period.' This gracious and elegant approach disguised at times his rapidity of scoring, especially in the pre-war years. His great year of 1937 witnessed some spectacular hitting, the most renowned being his 126 in 70 minutes against Kent at Canterbury, his century coming in 51 minutes, an innings which won him the Lawrence Trophy for the fastest hundred of the season. Against Gloucestershire at Bristol he struck the fastest fifty for Nottinghamshire, taking a mere fifteen minutes. Even his bigger innings were quick affairs, the first double-century of his career in England, 214* against Somerset, taking only 240 minutes. In August alone, he scored 1,150 runs; his season's aggregate of 2,540 runs placing him second to Hammond in the national averages, a position he again held in 1938. He had emerged as the county's leading batsman, heading the Nottinghamshire averages between 1935 and 1939. During this period, he made his Test debut in 1935 against South Africa, achieving little

Joe Hardstaff junior, one of the most elegant batsmen to have ever appeared for the county.

and being immediately dropped, a decision which Wisden's editor was to label 'astonishing'. By 1939 he was an established member of the England side, having played in all five Tests in the 1936/37 tour of Australia and having three Test centuries to his credit in sixteen appearances.

Hardstaff experienced a mixed 1946 season after his return from war service in India, failing to score 1,000 runs for the county for the only time between 1934 and 1952. In contrast, he scored 115 in the Test trial and an unbeaten 205* in the First Test at Lord's against India, captained the Players and was selected for his third tour of Australia in 1946/47. Not considered from the first as one of the prime batsmen, he appeared in only one Test.

Hardstaff showed all his old skill and form in 1947, scoring 2,396 runs and 7 hundreds, falling a few runs short of repeating his early feat of 1,000 runs in August; it was a month in which he scored three double-centuries and 2 hundreds. To the consternation of many, he was completely ignored by the selectors. He was selected to tour the West Indies the following winter under 'Gubby' Allen. Although Hardstaff had a successful series, he crossed swords with his captain, resenting the keep-fit classes and early-to-bed instructions from Allen: 'He had not gone through the war to be treated like a schoolboy.' Previous disagreements with Allen on the

1936/37 tour to Australia and his remark that Allen was a daft old clodpole did little to improve his Test chances. The story goes that Allen laid a £100 bet that Hardstaff would never play for England again. Hardstaff, after appearing at Trent Bridge in what was to be his last Test in 1948, tore up Allen's cheque.

There were to be a few final flourishes before he chose to retire at the age of forty-four in 1955. A wonderful season in 1949 saw him head the national batting averages with an average of 72.61. A century against Yorkshire marked a hundred against every first-class county and he also emulated his father's achievement – at last scoring a century in each innings of a match. His final record for the county was an impressive one: the most centuries for the county, 65; the second-highest aggregate of runs, 24,249; and 1,000 runs in a season for the county on twelve occasions. Only George Gunn has a better record. Hardstaff belongs to that select group of batsmen who have scored over 30,000 runs and but for the war would almost certainly have been one of the few to score a hundred centuries. However, he is probably best remembered for the manner in which he scored these runs rather than for the figures themselves. As his obituary in Wisden stated, 'In style he could stand comparison with the greatest exponents of the art of batsmanship.'

Born: 6 December 1907, Underwood, Nottinghamshire

Died: 8 August 1954, Nottingham

Batting

M	I	NO	Runs	HS
362	601	64	18823	239*
Ave	50	100	ct/st	
35.05	105	30	164	

Bowling

Runs	Wkts	Av	BB	5wI	10wM
8395	196	42.83	8-80	3	-

Best Performances
239* v. Hampshire, Nottingham, 1950
8-80 v. Lancashire, Manchester, 1931

It was once written of Charlie Harris that he was 'consistent only in inconsistency and unpredictability of conduct'. The inconsistency does not refer to his run-scoring, for he ended his career with a mid-thirties average, a figure steadily maintained throughout his career. Rarely striking the heights, he was never to experience a poor season. It was his approach to batting which baffled and at times exasperated both his team-mates and opponents. A sudden flurry of attacking strokes, often off the most accurate of deliveries, could be followed by a series of dead-bat shots to the most innocuous of half-volleys. His innings could be filled with the most beautifully executed strokes and ugly cross-bat shots. He was an incessant talker at the wicket, either to himself or to anyone who cared to listen. As Reg Simpson said, 'You never knew what he was going to do next.'

Hailing from North Nottinghamshire mining stock, Harris earned a regular first-team place in 1931. Thanks to a considerable number of not-outs, he ended the 1931 season at the head of the county's batting averages with an average of fifty and significantly opened the innings in the final match of the season. More sensationally, he took 8-80 against the 1930 Champions Lancashire in his second appearance, following this with 6-85 against Warwickshire. He never again produced bowling figures of this kind, with seventeen years passing before he claimed five wickets in an innings for a third and last time.

Welcomed by the local press as the find of the season, he was seen, aged twenty-two, as a future all-rounder, but it was his batting that won him a permanent place in the side. Between 1932 and 1939, he was ever-present in Championship games for five seasons, missing only seven games. A thousand-runs-a-season man, his most productive years were 1934 and 1937 when he struck over 1,800 runs. From 1932 he became part of the most successful opening partnership in the county's history, with Keeton figuring in 45 century opening stands, 15 of them realised over 150 runs. He was a perfect foil to the more aggressive Keeton, often going on to rescue his side after a poor start. He was twice to carry his bat: against Yorkshire in 1934 and against Hampshire in 1950, when with four wickets down for under ten, he made a career-best 239*. It was his second double-century, having scored 234 against Middlesex in 1933, after he and Keeton had put on 277 in 210 minutes.

After the Second World War, he began to be plagued by both injuries and illness, although still reaching 1,000 runs in three of his last six seasons. Giving way to Simpson as an opener, he left the county in 1951 and, although qualifying as a first-class umpire, was forced by ill-health to give up after only four appearances. He was to die before the season was over at the age of forty-five. A Nottinghamshire man to the core, his 362 first-class appearances were all for his county.

Michael John Harris
RHB & LB/WK, 1969-82

Born: 25 May 1944, St Just-in-Roseland, Cornwall

Batting

M	I	NO	Runs	HS
261	441	43	15308	201*
216	194	39	4755	104*

Ave	50	100	ct/st
38.46	89	35	242/14
30.67	3	25	128/6

Bowling

Runs	Wkts	Av	BB	5wI	10wM
3374	77	43.81	4-16	-	-
87	4	21.75	2-24	-	-

Best Performances
201* v. Glamorgan, Nottingham, 1973
104 v. Hampshire, Nottingham, 1970*
4-16 v. Warwickshire, Nottingham, 1969
2-24 v. Surrey, Nottingham, 1969

With the departure of Norman Hill during the 1968 season, Nottinghamshire were left without an experienced opening partner for Bolus. The vacancy was filled by the Middlesex opener Mike 'Pasty' Harris, who was to serve the county in a variety of roles in the next fourteen seasons: opening and middle-order batsman, leg-break bowler, wicketkeeper and occasional captain. Harris immediately proved his worth in his first season, making over 1,000 runs, his 149 against Leicestershire being the county's highest innings of that year.

In the next ten seasons, apart from his benefit year, 1977, when he suffered a complete loss of form, he consistently reached 1,000 runs, averaging over forty in six of them. In particular, he enjoyed two consecutive prolific seasons. Just missing 2,000 runs in 1970, he struck a century in all three competitions, being the first Nottinghamshire batsman to score a century in the John Player League. He had also struck up a successful opening partnership with Brian Bolus, the pair putting on 172 and 154 against Lancashire. Capped in that year, he surpassed himself in 1971, amassing 2,238 runs at an average of 50.86, one of only three batsmen to reach the 2,000 mark. He took third place in the national batting averages and headed the county's batting

averages for the only time. He became the only Nottinghamshire batsman to score two hundreds in a match twice in one season, something he again achieved in 1979, equalling George Gunn's record. Finishing the season on a high note with three consecutive hundreds in his last three Championship innings, something he had previously accomplished in May, he equalled Whysall's record of nine hundreds in a season for the county in six fewer innings.

Harris continued to bat consistently over the next eight seasons, 1977 apart, being four times the county's leading run-getter. He achieved a career-best 201* against Glamorgan in 1973, and also scored centuries against the West Indians and Indian tourists in 1973 and 1974 respectively. His fine performance in 1974, when he scored 1,690 runs, was thought by some to have warranted a place in the MCC party due to visit Australia in the winter.

He remained a regular member of the side for the remainder of the 1970s, taking on the role of vice-captain, reverting to the middle order for a time and keeping wicket till the arrival of French in 1977. He appeared infrequently during his last three seasons with the county, failing to score that one century against Gloucestershire, which would have given him a hundred against all seventeen first-class counties. He was appointed to the umpires' first-class list in 1998.

Born: 24 March 1944, Nairobi, Kenya

Batting

M	I	NO	Runs	HS
329	544	54	14355	182*
283	271	35	6806	120*
Ave	50	100	ct/st	
29.29	83	15	306/1	
28.83	36	4	121	

Bowling

Runs	Wkts	Av	BB	5wI	10wM
407	6	67.83	3-33	-	-
151	5	30.20	3-20	-	-

Best Performances

182* v. Gloucestershire, Nottingham, 1977
120* v. Warwickshire, Birmingham, 1981
3-33 v. Lancashire, Manchester, 1976
3-20 v. Durham, Chester-le-Street, 1967

In his eighteen-year-long playing career, 'Basher', as he quickly became known, remained a cheerful and popular figure on the county circuit. Immediately recognisable because of his extremely unorthodox crouching stance at the wicket, he proved to be a positive attacking middle-order batsman and one of the best cover points of his time. A safe pair of hands, his 306 catches is the highest number by a Nottinghamshire fielder since 1945. He was also called upon as an opening batsman and as an occasional wicketkeeper. His talent was recognised whilst appearing for an East African Invitation XI against the MCC touring side in 1963/64 and for Kenya. He arrived at Nottingham with the playing staff in a state of flux, as attempts were made to halt a depressing succession of results. He kept wicket in his debut game for the county in 1966 against Oxford University but it was as a batsman that he made his mark in 1967, scoring his maiden first-class hundred in his seventh Championship innings. His unbeaten 107 against Glamorgan, struck in 98 minutes, was at that time the fastest of the season. Unable to play in 1968, Sobers fulfilling the role of overseas player, Hassan returned to establish himself as a regular member of the side, being ever-present for the next three seasons. He reached 1,000 runs in a season for the first time in 1970. He enjoyed an amazing run of success against one particular county, Warwickshire, hitting 4 hundreds against that county in six years, three of them career-best innings at the time. Incredibly, he was to repeat these performances against the same county in

limited-overs cricket, averaging 100.62 in the John Player League, his 805 runs, including 3 hundreds, being the most by any county player against another county. His 120*, part of a first-wicket partnership of 188, was also a county record at that time, as was his 108 in 1979, the highest innings by a Notts 'keeper in that competition. For many years, he was the most successful limited-overs batsman for Nottinghamshire, being the first to reach 5,000 runs in the Sunday League in 1983.

Whilst his attacking play and his ability to keep wicket made him a vital asset in limited-overs cricket, he also proved a valuable member of the Championship side, reaching 1,000 runs on five occasions and heading the Notts batting averages in 1972, scoring more runs than any other batsman. In 1977 he scored a career-best 182 and a remarkable 106 against Kent when, after being injured in the first innings, he scored his second innings hundred, made in four hours with the aid of a runner; he was the only Nottinghamshire batsman to achieve this feat. He played a full part in the 1981 Championship-winning side, when he finished third in the county's batting averages. Retiring in 1985 to join the county's commercial staff, Hassan can look back on a career in which he has contributed entertainingly in a wide range of roles.

George Frank Henry Heane
LHB & RM, 1927-51

Born: 2 January 1904, Worksop, Nottinghamshire
Died: 24 October 1969, Skendleby, Lincolnshire

Batting

M	I	NO	Runs	HS
172	241	24	5854	138
Ave	**50**	**100**	**ct/st**	
26.97	30	9	93	

Bowling

Runs	Wkts	Av	BB	5wI	10wM
6532	201	32.49	6-52	4	1

Best Performances
138 v. Hampshire, Portsmouth, 1939
6-52 v. Hampshire, Nottingham, 1939

Whether George Heane would have experienced a lengthy first-class career is debatable, had it not been for a major crisis in the county's affairs at the close of the 1934 season. The removal of Arthur Carr led to the appointment of Heane as joint captain with another young amateur, Rhodes, for 1935.

Heane's amateur status appeared to be the major factor in his appointment, for Heane's previous playing record for the county was very ordinary. He was now called upon to lead a side containing a number of experienced professionals who were fiercely loyal to the man he had replaced in such controversial circumstances. Heane, to his credit, disarmed his critics in the best possible way. In his second home fixture against Kent, he hit an impressive 116 in only 135 minutes, putting on 105 for the eighth wicket with Larwood in 56 minutes; Notts winning by the impressive margin of 189 runs. The following home fixture against Somerset resulted in another century and a record 220 for the eighth wicket with R. Winrow. A few games later, two more hard-hitting innings against Essex resulted in two further century partnerships for the ninth and seventh wickets. His final batting average of 35, the consequence of some highly attractive innings, his splendid work in the field at cover point, and the county's rise of four places to finish fifth in the Championship, confirmed his position as sole captain in 1936. He was involved in a major incident in that year, leading his side off the field, claiming rain as the

reason, with Sussex requiring two runs for victory with all their wickets still intact. This preserved Nottinghamshire's unbeaten record, a popular move with his own players, but one which led to soured relations between the two counties for a time.

He was to retain the captaincy until 1946, in the process leading the side in 146 consecutive games, the longest consecutive run of appearances by a Nottinghamshire player. In all, he captained the side in 165 of his 172 appearances. He scored 9 hundreds in his six full seasons, his highest innings being 138 against Hampshire in 1939, one of three years in which he reached 1,000 runs. He never fulfilled his earlier promise as an all-rounder, partly the consequence of under-bowling himself. The only exception came in 1938, when his right-arm medium-pace claimed just over fifty wickets.

The end of his first-class career was as unexpected as its beginning. He was unexpectedly relieved of the captaincy prior to the commencement of the 1947 season, although there was talk of senior players being dissatisfied with his style of leadership. He did appear in four more games for the county, being recalled in 1951 at the age of forty-seven, thus becoming the oldest player to appear for the county in the post-war years. Whatever his shortcomings, Heane had captained the county in a time of change, when it was not yet apparent that the successful years of Nottinghamshire cricket were coming to an end.

Edward Ernest Hemmings
RHB & RM/OB, 1979-92

Born: 20 February 1949, Leamington Spa, Warwickshire

Batting

M	I	NO	Runs	HS
270	325	79	4366	127*
260	152	57	1354	43*

Ave	50	100	ct/st	
17.75	11	1	100	
14.25	-	-	62	

Bowling

Runs	Wkts	Av	BB	5wI	10wM
23681	850	27.86	7-23	43	8
8162	260	31.39	5-27	3	-

Best Performances
127* v. Yorkshire, Worksop, 1982
43 v. Northamptonshire, Northampton, 1979*
7-23 v. Lancashire, Nottingham, 1983
5-27 v. Gloucestershire, Nottingham, 1981

It was a stroke of great good fortune for the Nottinghamshire club that their search for experienced slow bowlers to create a more balanced attack should coincide with a disillusioned Warwickshire off-break bowler being prepared to start afresh with a new county. From his earliest involvement in the game, Hemmings had shown himself to be highly talented, joining the Warwickshire staff at sixteen after an excellent schoolboy career that had seen him captain an England Schoolboys XI. Initially a medium-pacer, he evolved into an accomplished off-spinner, capable of making useful runs.

Hemmings added another dimension to the county attack, shouldering the responsibility of bowling most overs, doing so eight times in his first nine seasons. He proved both a match-winner with his deceptive pace through the air and variable spin, and a bowler who could, if required, close up one end. Against his former county in 1987, he returned match figures of 10-77 off 72 overs, with 28 of his 32 overs in the first innings being maidens. He claimed most wickets for the county in his first two seasons, being capped in 1980. His importance to the side was underlined by the vital part he played in the two Championship successes in 1981 and 1987, taking 84 and 82 Championship wickets respectively in the two seasons. In 1981, in a crucial, closely-fought, penultimate fixture against local rivals Derbyshire, his match figures of 13-129 gave Notts a highly valuable 23 points. In the final fixture of 1987, his first innings figures of 5-12 and the important wicket of Maynard in the second contributed to an essential victory.

Other highlights of his Nottinghamshire career were: a hat-trick in 1984 against Northamptonshire, his most productive season in which he took 94 wickets; career-best Championship figures of 7-23 against Lancashire in 1983; and his only century, an unbeaten 127* against Yorkshire in 1982. For most Nottinghamshire followers, their most cherished moment of his stay with the county came with the last ball of the Benson & Hedges final against Essex, when facing Lever with nine fielders on the leg-side, he struck a fast yorker down past point for four to give Notts the trophy.

Hemmings' consistency – he took over fifty wickets in nine of his first ten seasons – was rewarded with sixteen Test appearances between 1982 and 1991, beginning with the wicket of Javed Miandad with only his fourth delivery in Test cricket, at his old home ground, Edgbaston. He toured Australia three times, twice heading the tour bowling averages and hitting a memorable 95 at Sydney after coming in as nightwatchman.

Hemmings was abruptly dismissed in 1992, but still proved his class by heading the bowling averages of his new county, Sussex, in the following season. A volatile character both on and off the field, he remained a highly popular cricketer during his years with the county, appreciated because he always gave his best and expected others to do the same.

Maurice Hill
RHB & LB, 1953-65

Born: 14 September 1935, Scunthorpe, Lincolnshire

Batting

M	I	NO	Runs	HS
237	394	32	8977	137*
4	4	0	119	107
Ave	**50**	**100**	**ct/st**	
24.79	44	7	123	
29.75	-	1	5	

Bowling

Runs	Wkts	Av	BB	5wI	10wM
305	5	61.00	2-60	-	-

Best Performances

137* v. Lancashire, Worksop, 1961
107 v. Somerset, Taunton, 1964
2-60 v. West Indians, Nottingham, 1957

Statistics are often a useful guide to a cricketer's performance, but occasionally do not tell the whole story of a player's contribution to the game. This is certainly the case with Maurice Hill's career; a total of only 7 hundreds in 292 first-class innings and a final average of 24 are unimpressive for a player who made his debut in the mid-1950s and continued into the early 1970s. The very fact that he was persevered with for so long and that two other counties were prepared to take him on after his spell with Nottinghamshire suggest a promise of great things, which were never realised. From the first he always looked a good player and throughout his career produced a number of brilliant innings.

At seventeen, one of the youngest players to make his first-class debut for the county, Hill made a solitary appearance in 1953, but was then obliged to lose two years whilst completing his National Service. In 1957, still only twenty-one, he impressed many critics with his natural talent as a batsman, appearing in 24 out of the 28 Championship games and scoring over 1,000 runs in his first full season. Beginning with 85 against Northamptonshire, an innings described as elegant and full of attractive strokes, his first six innings yielded 365 runs, including 50 against the West Indians and a rapid 95 in 120 minutes against Worcestershire, which contained 2 sixes

and 13 fours. Just short of his maiden hundred, he went down the wicket to Jenkins and was stumped, an indication of the manner in which he played. He achieved very little of note during the remainder of the season, but many believed that here was the natural successor to Hardstaff and Simpson. It was not to be.

Persevered with in 1958, when he scored his maiden first-class hundred and again reached 1,000 runs, he subsequently failed to secure a permanent place in the side until mid-June 1961. Again he produced a number of brilliant innings: 90 in even time against Gloucestershire, 76 runs coming in boundaries, and 105 in 120 minutes against Warwickshire. He was capped by the county in that year, having recorded 3 hundreds and 1,215 runs. It was to be the only season he was to average over thirty. For the next three seasons, he reached his 1,000 runs as a permanent member of the side, runs of low scores being interspersed with innings of real quality: in 1963, an unbeaten 100 in even time, containing 4 sixes and 12 fours against Warwickshire; in 1964, 6 sixes and 4 fours in 77 against Derbyshire, and 72 in boundaries out of an unbeaten 90 against Surrey. In the Gillette Cup, against Somerset, his 107 contained 70 runs in boundaries.

One year later, and still only thirty, he was released by the county, twice attempting to resurrect his career with Derbyshire and Somerset but eventually retiring in 1971. His legacy was a number of cameo innings of the highest quality, and memories of his outstanding fielding in the covers.

Norman Wilfred Hill
LHB & LB, 1953-68

Born: 22 August 1935, Holbeck, Nottinghamshire

Batting

M	I	NO	Runs	HS
280	513	32	14036	201*
7	7	0	165	66

Ave	50	100	ct/st	
29.18	61	22	224	
23.57	1	-	2	

Bowling

Runs	Wkts	Av	BB	5wl	10wM
261	2	130.50	1-28	-	-

Best Performances
201* v. Sussex, Shireoaks, Worksop, 1961
66 v. Wiltshire, Nottingham, 1965
1-28 v. Northamptonshire, Nottingham, 1959

A chapter in Peter Wynne-Thomas's book *Trent Bridge* is entitled 'Barren Days 1958-67', a decade which almost encapsulates Norman Hill's Nottinghamshire career. During this era of post-Dooland and pre-Sobers, the county was to occupy one of the bottom three Championship places on ten occasions, five of them in last position. It was a time when the county's cricketers required a strong character and broad shoulders, and Norman Hill certainly fitted that description, both physically and mentally. A short, stocky individual, he was described as being 'built like a barrel'; he developed into a tenacious left-hand opening batsman.

Unathletic in appearance and not the most graceful of batsman, what he lacked in elegance, he made up for with determination and application. Despite his bulk, he was also a fine fielder close to the wicket, and is high on the list of the county's most successful fielders. Hill made his first-class debut in 1953, aged 17 years 316 days, the fifth youngest player to appear for the county in the twentieth century. However, he did not gain a permanent place in the side until 1958.

By the end of 1958, Hill had established himself as Reg Simpson's opening partner, his 153 against Kent being the county's highest innings of the season. His 1,000 runs that year was the first of seven for the county, these being the only ones in which he played a full season. This consistent form included two exceptional years, 1959 and 1961, his fine run of form being interrupted in 1960 when he missed thirteen games

after sustaining a broken bone in the hand. In both seasons, he registered over 2,000 runs in county matches alone, one of only nine batsmen to do so for the county. He was capped in 1959 after scoring a century in both innings against Lancashire, all the sweeter as he had suffered a pair against Statham in their previous encounter.

The year 1961 brought a career-best, unbeaten 201* against Sussex and was to prove his most successful year, his aggregate of 2185 runs at 40.86 putting him at the top of the Nottinghamshire batting averages for the only time in his career. In 1962 he scored over 500 more runs than any other Nottinghamshire batsman, enjoying a fine run of success in June, making eight scores of fifty or over in ten consecutive innings. This included a remarkable pair of innings at Eastbourne, when after hitting 193 in the first innings, he carried his bat in the second for 23*, as Notts were shot out for a total of 57.

Hill retired at the end of the 1962 season but returned in mid-season, going on to accept the captaincy in 1966. With Sobers assuming the captaincy in 1968, Hill decided to call it a day, still aged only thirty-two, thus denying himself a few years with a successful team. Popular with both his team-mates and spectators alike, he had given his best in the most dispiriting of times for the county.

James Iremonger
RHB & RM, 1899-1914

Born: 5 March 1876, Norton, Yorkshire
Died: 25 March 1956, West Bridgford, Nottingham

Batting

M	I	NO	Runs	HS
315	507	60	16110	272
Ave	**50**	**100**	**ct/st**	
36.04	80	31	165	

Bowling

Runs	Wkts	Av	BB	5wI	10wM
13350	596	22.39	8-21	34	8

Best Performances
272 v. Kent, Nottingham, 1904
8-21 v. Gloucestershire, Nottingham, 1912

J. IREMONGER.
(NOTTINGHAM)

James Iremonger, although overshadowed by some of his well-known contemporaries, was one of Nottinghamshire's most successful players with both bat and ball. He is one of only three players to score over 10,000 runs and take over 500 wickets.

Iremonger began his career with Notts essentially as a batsman, qualifying for the county as a child of Nottinghamshire parents. He made his debut in 1899, the turning point in his career coming in the county's ignominious performance against Yorkshire in 1901, when Notts were dismissed for 13. Asked to open in the second innings, Iremonger carried his bat for 55*, and a new opening partnership with A.O. Jones was born. Iremonger went on to enjoy a phenomenal August, scoring hundreds in four consecutive matches. His maiden century, 119 against Surrey at The Oval, also heralded a new first for the county, he and Jones putting on a hundred for the first wicket in both innings. A 238 partnership against Essex and a stand of 119 against Derbyshire followed next. Between 1901 and 1911, they shared 25 century opening partnerships, averaging 41.65 in their 229 opening partnerships. They repeated the feat of putting on a hundred in each innings when they added 102 and 303 against Gloucestershire at Trent Bridge in 1902.

As a batsman, Iremonger continued to go from strength to strength, and he was named as one of *Wisden*'s Five Cricketers of the Year in 1903. Standing over 6ft tall and physically strong, he possessed infinite patience, often playing the anchor role in an innings. In 1904 he topped the county batting averages, scoring 1,949 runs for the county, the highest number by a Nottinghamshire batsman at that time. During June, he scored 1,010 runs at an average of 101.00, making 6 hundreds – 3 in consecutive innings – and hitting a career-best 272 against Kent, one of his 4 double-hundreds for the county. He also carried his bat for the second time, making 189* out of 377 against Middlesex.

Circumstances in 1908 gave him new opportunities as a bowler when he headed the county's bowling averages. His steady, accurate medium-slow bowling brought him over 90 wickets in 1911, 1912 and 1913; his best figures were 8-21 against Gloucestershire in 1912, this including three wickets in four balls. By 1914 he was the side's best all-rounder, scoring over 1,000 runs and taking 74 wickets. He was selected for the MCC tour of Australia in 1911/12 as a bowler, although he was not chosen for any of the five Tests.

Elder brother of Albert, the idiosyncratic Notts County goalkeeper, James himself was a highly successful footballer, playing for Nottingham Forest and England, and eventually becoming player-manager of Notts County.

Iremonger was the Nottinghamshire coach from 1921 to 1938. Harold Larwood was full of praise for his work, commenting that 'if anyone has got a spark of cricket in him, old Jimmy will fan it into something like a fire.'

John Jackson

RHB & RF (round-arm), 1855-66

Born: 21 May 1833, Bungay, Suffolk
Died: 4 November 1901, Brownlow Hill, Liverpool

Batting

M	I	NO	Runs	HS
33	52	5	719	100
Ave	**50**	**100**	**ct/st**	
15.29	3	1	27	

Bowling

Runs	Wkts	Av	BB	5wI	10wM
1932	136+5	14.20	9-49	10	2

Best Performances

100 v. Kent, Cranbrook, 1863
9-49 v. Surrey, The Oval, 1860

John Jackson (pictured centre) was a man of impressive physique, standing over 6ft tall and weighing about 14st, who developed into the fastest round-arm bowler of his day. His great pace allied to his accuracy generated a succession of stories and anecdotes about the 'Demon Bowler', a reputation about which Jackson was only too pleased to elaborate. He was often referred to as 'Foghorn', the consequence of his habit of blowing his nose loudly whenever he claimed a wicket. Such was his fame that he became the first cricketer to appear in a cartoon in *Punch*. Most of the best batsmen of the day considered him the most difficult fast bowler they had ever stood against, remarking on his easy action, his stamina, his command over the ball and his ability to vary his pitch and pace, whilst his armoury was said to include both the yorker and the beamer.

Born in Suffolk, he had been brought to Nottinghamshire within a week of his birth, learning his cricket at Southwell. His forty wickets for a variety of sides against Clarke's All-England XI persuaded Clarke to include him in the Nottinghamshire XI in 1855. This was the first of thirty-three appearances for Nottinghamshire, for whom he was an automatic choice until his final season. Two outstanding performances stood out. The first came in 1860, against Surrey at The Oval, when bowling unchanged in both innings he claimed match figures of 15-73, his second innings analysis being 9-49, becoming only the second bowler to have taken nine wickets in an innings for the county. Three years later he achieved a marvellous all-round performance at Cranbrook against Kent, when batting at number eight, he scored the only century of his career, adding 109 for the eighth wicket with R.C. Tinley, and then bowling unchanged in both innings with James

Grundy to complete a fine match with figures of 12-43. It marked the first occasion a player had scored a century and taken over ten wickets in a match for the county. It was also the first time two Nottinghamshire bowlers had bowled unchanged throughout both innings of a match.

Jackson was virtually an automatic choice for the North and the Players, as well as the AEE, for whom he made 252 appearances, taking an estimated 2,187 wickets, returning incredible match figures of 22-35 against XXII of Uppingham, and 10-1 against XXII of Cornwall. Twice, he took over 100 wickets in important matches, his best year being 1860 when his 109 wickets cost 9.20 runs apiece. Between 1858 and 1860, he took nine wickets in an innings on three occasions. Jackson participated in two overseas tours: George Parr's team's visit to North America in 1859 during which Jackson took 10-10 against XXII of USA; and to Australia and New Zealand in 1863/64.

By 1865 the amount of bowling he had been called upon to do began to take its toll, and a leg injury in 1865 ended his county career that year. He continued playing for a variety of clubs at a lower level throughout the country, even appearing as a first-class umpire in 1884, but ended his days in the workhouse at Liverpool. It was a sad end to a career in which he had failed only once in 115 games to take a wicket in both innings of a match and this in his penultimate game. He was 'always straight, always great, always to be feared'.

Arthur Jepson
RHB & RFM, 1938-59

Born: 12 July 1915, Selston, Nottinghamshire
Died: 17 July 1997, Kirkby-in-Ashfield,
 Nottinghamshire

Batting

M	I	NO	Runs	HS
390	531	88	6351	130
Ave	50	100	ct/st	
14.33	11	1	201	

Bowling

Runs	Wkts	Av	BB	5wI	10wM
30510	1050	29.05	8-45	40	6

Best Performances
130 v. Worcestershire, Nottingham, 1950
8-45 v. Leicestershire, Nottingham, 1958

Just as Keeton and Harris became inextricably linked in the minds of supporters in the immediate post-war years, so were the names of Butler and Jepson, who came together for the first time as the county's opening attack in the first Championship fixture of the 1946 season, and whose partnership lasted until May 1954. As with Keeton and Harris, they were to complement each other: Butler was essentially a bowler of real pace, and Jepson a fast medium-pace stock bowler. Both, however, shared several important qualities. Both bowled their hearts out for the county at a time when everything was against them. With a pitch entirely unsuited to their bowling, and little support forthcoming from the remainder of the attack, they were both overbowled but stuck to their task with great determination.

Jepson began his Nottinghamshire career five years after Butler, his first two appearances coinciding with Larwood's final two games. Before the war he operated as first change, but in 1946 took over as one of the county's opening bowlers, remaining as such until his final game against Sussex in 1959. Apart from a spate of injuries between 1949 and 1951, he was virtually an ever-present in the side throughout his long career. His best season came in 1947 when he captured over a hundred wickets for the only time, at the same time averaging over twenty-two with the bat. Equally impressive was his tally of 1,154 overs for the county, the highest number bowled by a Nottinghamshire bowler since 1927 and still the most bowled in a season by a

pace bowler for the county. No other bowler since the war can equal Jepson's record of taking over fifty or more wickets in a season on eleven occasions. Five times in his fourteen seasons after the war, he was to claim most wickets in a season for the county. Although his partnership with Butler ended in 1954, at the age of forty-one, in 1956, he recorded his best match figures of 12-120 against Warwickshire. His last full season, 1958, saw him take his 1,000th wicket for the county, claim his best first-class figures, 8-45 against Leicestershire, and top the county's bowling averages – a tribute to his fitness and enthusiasm at the age of forty-three.

Jepson was one of only twelve Notts players to take over 500 wickets and score over 5,000 runs, often contributing useful and usually quick runs batting at number eight. Against Yorkshire in 1952, he struck 4 consecutive sixes off Johnnie Wardle. His one century came in 1950, his 130 against Worcestershire including 4 sixes and 13 fours, adding 270 for the sixth wicket with Simpson. He possessed a safe pair of hands, often fielding at gully and short-leg, evident in the 201 catches he held. He stood in for Simpson as captain between 1954 and 1959, leading the county on thirty-five occasions, the most by a non-designated captain. His ability to maintain his form and fitness well into his forties was clearly assisted by his career as a professional footballer, Jepson keeping goal for Port Vale, Stoke City and Lincoln City between 1938 and 1950. He is the only sportsman to appear in over 100 Football League games and to take over 1,000 first-class wickets. After retirement, he became a first-class umpire, retiring in 1984 after twenty-five seasons, having stood in four Tests.

Paul Johnson
RHB & RM, 1982-2002

Born: 24 April 1965, Newark, Nottinghamshire

Batting

M	I	NO	Runs	HS
365	614	60	20256	187
385	363	45	10135	167*
Ave	**50**	**100**	**ct/st**	
36.56	116	40	233/1	
31.87	57	13	113	

Bowling

Runs	Wkts	Av	BB	5wI	10wM
617	6	102.83	1-9	-	-
23	1	23.00	1-2	-	-

Best Performances
Batting: 187 v. Lancashire, Manchester, 1993
167 v. Kent, Nottingham, 1993*
Bowling: 1-9 v. Cambridge University,
  Nottingham, 1984
1-2 v. Northamptonshire, Nottingham, 2001

'Johno' entered club cricket at a ridiculously early age, and had graduated to representative schools elevens, England Schoolboys and England Young Cricketers, by the age of seventeen. At 17 years and 77 days, he became the youngest Nottinghamshire batsman to make his Championship debut. On his fifteenth Championship appearance, playing against Gloucestershire at Bristol in 1983, he scored 125 – the youngest Nottinghamshire batsman to score a century, aged 18 years 128 days. His next landmark came in 1985 when, at twenty years of age, he became the youngest batsman to reach 1,000 Championship runs for the county, achieving this in style with an unbeaten 120 against Lancashire in 137 minutes. Another first was an undefeated 101 against Staffordshire on his debut in the NatWest competition, which won him the Man of the Match award. In 1987, at the age of only twenty-two, he won a Championship medal, being ever-present and scoring more runs than any other Nottinghamshire batsman.

He had already established his reputation as an aggressive middle-order batsman, who on his day was capable of destroying the opposition bowling. Short and stocky, he dealt severely with anything short, excelling at the pull over mid-wicket and the square cut. Such a positive approach to batting produced some exhilarating performances. His unbeaten 107 against Warwickshire in 1992 in 52 minutes was the fourth-fastest hundred for Nottinghamshire. It is almost impossible to discover a slow innings amongst his 40 hundreds for the county, his longest stay at the wicket being his career-best

187 against Lancashire, which took 381 minutes. Even then, he struck 2 sixes and 22 fours. Such a forceful approach naturally lent itself to limited-overs cricket. In 1990 alone, he recorded 4 hundreds, three in the Sunday League taking between 71 and 97 balls. His most impressive limited-overs innings was his unbeaten 167 against Kent at Trent Bridge in 1993, which included 7 sixes and 20 fours and took 106 balls.

A permanent fixture in the Notts XI until his retirement in 2002, he reached 1,000 runs on nine occasions. Three of his least productive years came when he led the side from 1996 to halfway through the 1998 season. It was surely no coincidence that the day after resigning the captaincy, he hit 100 in 98 balls against Northamptonshire.

Representative honours were to evade Johnson. He toured with England A to Bermuda and the West Indies in 1991/92, and was chosen for the following winter tour to Australia, only to be prevented by injury from taking part. Many would consider his positive batting worthy of at least a place in an England limited-overs side. He deservedly reached the target of 20,000 runs for the county in his final season, becoming one of only three Nottinghamshire batsmen to also score 10,000 runs in limited-overs matches.

Born: 16 August 1872, Shelton, Nottinghamshire
Died: 21 December 1914, Dunstable, Bedfordshire

Batting

M	I	NO	Runs	HS
397	648	35	20244	296
Ave	50	100	ct/st	
33.02	108	30	466/1	

Bowling

Runs	Wkts	Av	BB	5wI	10wM
9449	294	32.13	8-71	7	-

Best Performances
296 v. Gloucestershire, Nottingham, 1903
8-71 v. Gloucestershire, Nottingham, 1911

The first Nottinghamshire captain to lead a Championship-winning side after the County Championship assumed its modern form was A.O. Jones in 1907; it was his eighth season as captain, a position he was to retain until his death in 1914. He was to lead the county on 282 occasions, still the second-highest number in the county's history.

It was whilst at Cambridge University, for whom he made his first-class debut, that he first appeared for the county in 1892. *Wisden* was impressed, commenting that here was a batsman of high promise, who was 'quite irreproachable in the field'. It was essentially for his fielding ability that Jones was awarded his Blue the following year, a talent that won him acclaim throughout his playing career. After a magnificent left-handed catch in the Birmingham Test of 1909, Pelham Warner was to write, 'How positively glorious it must be to field like the Notts captain.' He was especially noted for his magnificent catching close to the wicket, especially in the slip and gully area, the latter allegedly invented by Jones. Nottinghamshire's most successful bowler, Wass, could be grateful to Jones, who was to hold 137 catches off Wass. Jones' tally of 466 catches is still a record number for the county as is his total of twenty-five or more catches in a season on ten occasions. He also shares with Voce a record of seven catches in a match. His example alone inspired others, and under his leadership the county emerged as a superb fielding side.

His captaincy was equally inspiring, based more on his personal qualities than on his tactical skill. All speak of his keenness and enthusiasm, his ability to lift a side and his refusal to accept defeat. His personality was also reflected in his approach to batting. Essentially he was a positive player, who enjoyed striking the ball and making his runs quickly. His stance was an unattractive one, but his crouch over the bat with knees bent and legs astride as the bowler approached failed to impede his more forceful strokes. He was especially noted for his off-side shots, especially the square off-drive and a powerful cut, 'as if he were chopping a man's head off'. Described as a 'dasher', his natural inclination to play his shots and take on the bowling often cost him his wicket and made for inconsistency, but this was balanced by a determination to occupy the crease when necessary. He was to pass 150 on nine occasions with his four double-centuries all over 249, his highest innings of 296 in 1903 being the highest innings at that time for the county. In the same year, he became the first Notts batsman to score a century before lunch on the first day, a feat he repeated in 1911 – the only Notts batsman to achieve this on two occasions.

Jones also had his moments as a bowler, although his leg-break bowling did tend to be expensive. Against Gloucestershire in 1909, he

A.O. Jones, who led Nottinghamshire to the 1907 title, alongside two other county captains, W.G. Grace of Gloucestershire and D.L.A. Jephson of Surrey.

county was dismissed for 13, at that time the lowest total in Championship history. Jones, who recorded the highest score – 4 – decided to open with Iremonger in the second, the forerunner of 229 such partnerships, which were to yield 25 century opening stands. One of their most memorable achievements came in this first year, when they became the first opening Notts pair to make over a hundred runs in each innings, a feat they were to repeat in 1904. Both were memorable: the first against Surrey being the pair's initial century partnership, the second involving a second innings stand of 303.

took 8-71 to win the game, becoming one of only five Nottinghamshire players to score both a double-century and take eight wickets in an innings for the county.

His county career developed slowly, Jones scoring his first fifty after thirty-nine games, and it was not until 1899 that he, as *Wisden* put it, 'realised the hopes of his friends ... as one of the great batsmen of the day'. Reaching 1,000 runs for the first time, something he was to accomplish on seven further occasions, he averaged over fifty in the Championship. He participated in a record first-wicket partnership of 391 with Shrewsbury, was chosen as one of *Wisden*'s Five Cricketers of the Year, and made his Test debut against Australia. In 1901 Jones achieved 2,000 runs in all games, complemented by over fifty wickets and over thirty catches. His 1,718 runs for the county was also the most by any Nottinghamshire batsman in a season at that time. He was, *Wisden* reported, emphatically an England cricketer.

By this time, Jones had become part of one of the most successful opening partnerships in the county's history. The partnership began in one of the most abject performances in the county's history. Against Yorkshire at Trent Bridge, the

He was, however, unable to carry his county form into the Test arena. He experienced a miserable 1901/02 tour of Australia, averaging only ten in his five Test appearances. His subsequent visit in 1907/08, this time as captain, was equally unfortunate, illness permitting him to play in only two Tests. At home, although scoring hundreds against the Australians for the county in both 1905 and 1909 to become the first Nottinghamshire batsman to do so, he lasted only two Tests in both series.

At county level, his inspiring leadership was a key factor in the Championship success of 1907, but after suffering bronchial problems on the Australian tour, his remaining career was to be affected by similar health problems, a situation not helped by his heavy smoking. Ironically, he was remarkably injury-free, missing only four games through injury between 1895 and 1912. He was also an excellent rugby player, appearing 224 times for Leicester as full-back or three-quarter and later becoming an international referee. In 1913 his health dramatically deteriorated and playing in only a handful of games subsequently, he died of consumption in December 1914, at the age of forty-two.

William Walter Keeton
RHB, 1926-52

Born: 30 April 1905, Shirebrook, Derbyshire
Died: 10 October 1980, Forest Town,
   Nottinghamshire

Batting

M	I	NO	Runs	HS
382	633	42	23744	312*
Ave	50	100	ct/st	
40.17	117	54	74	

Bowling

Runs	Wkts	Av	BB	5wl	10wM
103	2	51.50	2-16	-	-

Best Performances
312* v. Middlesex, The Oval, 1939
2-16 v. Sussex, Horsham, 1934

Yet another player from a North Nottingham-shire colliery side, Keeton joined the staff in 1925, only securing a regular first XI place in 1931. By the end of that season, he had scored over 1,000 Championship runs and received his county cap. His total of over 2,000 runs and 6 Championship hundreds in both of the following two seasons confirmed earlier opinions that he was another exceptional Nottinghamshire opening batsman. His aggregate of 2,112 runs in 1933 was the fourth-highest for the county. It included a great run of form in August, when he scored 1,102 runs in 15 innings, striking 6 hundreds, 3 in consecutive innings. Against Yorkshire at Bradford, he scored 110 before lunch on the first day, only the second Notts batsman to achieve this feat. A similar run of form in 1937 saw him score 3 centuries and 2 nineties in eight games, one of the latter being an unbeaten 99* when he carried his bat against Kent, the last man being run out going for a quick single. In 1949, aged forty-four, he again scored 3 consecutive hundreds in a run of 4 centuries in five innings. Two of these were double-hundreds; his 208 against Glamorgan at Trent Bridge being his fiftieth three-figure innings and his seventh double-century, at that time the highest number by a Nottinghamshire player. He was the oldest bats-man to have scored a double-century for the county.

He appeared in only two Tests, against Australia in 1934 and against the West Indies in 1939. Consolation came in his 312* against Middlesex, the only triple-century ever to be scored for the county, and his selection as one of Wisden's Five Cricketers of the Year.

After the war, he continued to maintain a consistently high standard, culminating in a magnificent 1949 season when he scored over 2,000 runs at an average of 55.37, standing sev-enth in the national batting averages. Two years earlier he had become the first Nottinghamshire batsman to score a century against every first-class county, the same year in which he was to receive a record Nottinghamshire benefit. In 1950, with Harris, he completed the last of their 45 century opening partnerships, the highest number in the county's history. They shared cen-tury opening partnerships in both innings against Northamptonshire, repeating their feat of seven-teen years earlier against Kent. Keeton's highest opening stand was 318 in 315 minutes, with Simpson against Lancashire in 1949, their fourth century partnership in consecutive games.

Keeton's contribution to Nottinghamshire cricket is obvious from the county records: the third-highest number of centuries; the third-high-est run-scorer; and the second highest in Championship matches. Above all, Keeton is remembered for his positive approach to batting. A fine, attacking, elegant batsman, relying on technique rather than physical strength, his trademark was the on-drive, supported by fine cutting and a good cover drive. Quick on his feet and very fast between the wickets, he was a delight to watch.

Born: 14 November 1904, Nuncargate, Nottinghamshire
Died: 22 July 1995, Sydney, Australia

Batting

M	I	NO	Runs	HS
300	372	66	6137	102*
Ave	**50**	**100**	**ct/st**	
20.05	20	3	203	

Bowling

Runs	Wkts	Av	BB	5wI	10wM
20253	1247	16.24	9-41	89	19

Best Performances
102* v. Sussex, Nottingham, 1931
9-41 v. Kent, Nottingham, 1931

Harold Larwood's association with Bodyline was to overshadow his reputation as the greatest fast bowler of his decade, and one of the best in the history of the game. From 1927 to 1936, he headed the national bowling averages on five occasions, a record which no other fast bowler in England can match. His average of 16.29 in Championship matches is staggering, only three other pace bowlers returning a lower one.

Another graduate from the North Nottinghamshire coalfields, his rise to the top was a rapid one, for on his thirty-fifth first-class appearance, he was selected to play against Australia at Lord's in 1926, his first victim being the great C.G. Macartney. On joining the Trent Bridge staff, doubts were expressed as to whether he had the physique to sustain a first-class career as a fast bowler, a forecast which was to contain an element of truth, for he was to appear in only 21 of the 45 Tests played during his international career, his absences often the consequence of injury or illness. Standing only 5ft 8in and weighing about 10 ½st, he did, however, possess strong leg and back muscles and was to

subsequently fill out to about 12st. He was helped in two other vital respects. His development as a bowler was supervised by the great Nottinghamshire coach, Jimmy Iremonger, whilst his captain, Arthur Carr, seeing his potential as a strike bowler, resisted the temptation to over-bowl him in his formative years, using him essentially in short spells of about four overs, with intervals of 30 to 60 minutes rest.

Contemporaries describe his technique as being as good as any fast bowler's could be: a smooth, controlled run-up of about eighteen paces, gradually accelerating as he approached the wicket; a perfectly-balanced high overhead, sideways action with a huge body swing and a follow-through, which when bowling flat out, often ended with his knuckles scraping the turf. Allied to his extreme pace was a very high level of accuracy and an ability at times to bring the ball back sharply from the off. A final wristy movement gave him pace and lift off the wicket. He relished his role as a bowler who was capable of demoralising opposing batsmen. 'It was nice', he once remarked, 'to be master of a batsman.' When teamed up with Bill Voce, they became the most feared opening bowlers in the country, being the last Nottinghamshire pair of bowlers to bowl unchanged throughout a match, when they shared all twenty wickets against Leicestershire in 1932.

Larwood headed the national averages in both 1927 and 1928, and was an obvious selection for the 1928/29 tour to Australia, where he made an immediate impact with 6-32 on a near-perfect pitch in the opening Test. He appeared in all five Tests in the series, a tribute to Chapman who never overworked him. He was to play in only one other complete Test series, the Australian tour of 1932/33. Illness also restricted his opportunities and effectiveness in the 1930 home series against Australia. In his book *Bodyline*, he was to write, 'my health was not of the best up to the end of 1930' and later that 'after an operation in 1930 put right the internal trouble, I have been a different bowler'. Doubts about his fitness to tour Australia in 1932/33 were, however, dispelled by his county form in both 1931 and 1932; in a wet 1931 season, he claimed 129 wickets at a mere 12.03 apiece, including a career-best 9-41 against Kent, and followed this with his most productive season, taking 162 wickets at 12.86 apiece.

Larwood proved an ideal bowler for Jardine's strategy for the 1932/33 series. His great pace, accuracy and control brought him a record 33 wickets for a fast bowler in this series and he took Bradman's wicket on six occasions on the tour. He was to bowl as many or more overs than any other England bowler in seven out of the ten Australian innings. His exertions on the hard Australian wickets finally told. In the ultimate innings of the series, he was forced to limp off with a fractured toe. It was the end of both his Test career and his period as a great fast bowler. He bowled only ten overs in 1933, appearing for the county purely as a batsman, but with a shorter run-up and bowling fast medium, his great technique enabled to head the national bowling averages for one last time in 1936, a year which brought him a record benefit of £2,098.

Hopes that he would appear against Australia in 1934 were dashed by the failed, unpublicised attempts to secure an apology from Larwood regarding his newspaper article stating he would never again play against the Australians. He was too proud a man to apologise for his part in the Bodyline series. Talking to his mother about his decision not to sign a letter of apology, she replied, 'If you do sign, you'll never see me again.'

Harold Larwood was a highly talented cricketer in every aspect of the game, an excellent fielder and a straight hard-hitting batsman, who could have become a successful all-rounder if his bowling had not taken precedence. He scored three first-class hundreds, one of which came in a match in which he also claimed 6-38. Another involved a tenth-wicket partnership of 136 in 55 minutes with Bill Voce. His last Test innings of 98 was the highest Test innings at that time by a night-watchman.

Cheered off the field by an Australian crowd, he was to receive an equally warm reception when he emigrated to Australia in 1950. Amends were also made in England. He was made an honorary member of the MCC in 1948, and was belatedly awarded the MBE in 1993. It was the least that could be done for a man who, as Cardus wrote, 'wore himself out in the service of his country'.

Harold Larwood, the most feared fast bowler to have played for the county.

Clairmonte Christopher Lewis
RHB & RFM, 1992-95

Born: 14 February 1968, Georgetown, Guyana

Batting

M	I	NO	Runs	HS
37	58	10	2256	247
41	34	4	802	89
Ave	50	100	ct/st	
47.00	11	5	36	
26.73	4	-	11	

Bowling

Runs	Wkts	Av	BB	5wI	10wM
3552	127	27.96	6-90	4	1
1479	49	30.18	5-46	1	-

Best Performances
247 v. Durham, Chester-le-Street, 1993
89 v. Northumberland, Jesmond, 1994
6-90 v. Surrey, Nottingham, 1992
5-46 v. Kent, Nottingham, 1992

The signing of the two highly promising young all-rounders, the New Zealander Chris Cairns and the former Leicestershire and current England player Chris Lewis, for the 1992 season appeared a major coup for the new manager John Birch. Scyld Berry in *Wisden* observed that 'there seemed little that Lewis, at the age of twenty-four, could not accomplish'. Many saw him as the long-term answer to England's search for an all-rounder, a fast bowler with growing promise as a talented explosive mid-order batsman, coupled with an outstanding ability in the field. There was little to complain about in his first year with the county. In only his second appearance, he emphasised his match-winning qualities, his unbeaten 134* and innings figures of 5-74 against Northamptonshire contributing to a three-wicket victory. Later in the year, he played a significant part in the defeat of Surrey with match figures of 10-155 and 76 runs for once out. Second in the county's batting averages and first in the bowling, little more could have been asked of Lewis.

His second season was far less impressive. His county aggregate of 577 runs was mainly the consequence of his 247, the highest of the English season, against Durham in early September. It was the highest innings played by a Nottinghamshire batsman since 1951 and contributed to a county-record seventh-wicket partnership of 301 with French. His late show of form again brought him Test recognition, Lewis being selected for the 1993/94 tour of the West Indies.

On paper, 1995 was his most successful with the county, Lewis heading both the batting and bowling averages, scoring more runs and taking more wickets than in his previous two seasons. Once again, a late burst of form in the closing stages of the season aroused scepticism that his major concern was selection for England's winter tour. This run included an unbeaten 220* against Warwickshire and, in what proved to be his final innings for the county, an undefeated 108* against Middlesex. His relationship with the county deteriorated, Lewis expressing a wish to be released to join a London county and complaining that the award of his county cap was long overdue. In 1995, after injury had restricted his appearances to four limited-overs matches, Nottinghamshire agreed in mid-season to release him from his six-year contract. The Nottinghamshire crowd greeted the announcement during the match against Yorkshire with applause, an indication of how far his standing had fallen.

Statistically, Lewis achieved one of the best batting records with the county, but he made only thirty-four Championship appearances in four seasons. Injuries and Test calls played their part, but he never convinced the membership that he was totally committed to the county's cause. As with his other county clubs and his country, he never fulfilled the promise of his undoubted talent.

Born: 11 February 1894, Kimberley,
  Nottinghamshire
Died: 4 August 1950, Forest Fields, Nottingham

Batting

M	I	NO	Runs	HS
369	507	79	10473	124
Ave	50	100	ct/st	
24.46	43	7	649/132	

Bowling

Runs	Wkts	Av	BB	5wl	10wM
27	0	-	-	-	-

Best Performances
124 v. Warwickshire, Nottingham, 1936

Ben Lilley made his debut for the county in 1921 as a temporary opening batsman but it was not until 1925 that he could claim to be the county's first-choice 'keeper. Until then he was kept out by the veteran Oates, now in his late forties, However, after an unbeaten 200 for the Second XI against Staffordshire, against the legendary Sidney Barnes, he at last replaced Oates on a regular basis at the relatively late age of thirty-one. Like his predecessor, he went on to monopolise the position for many years, one of only three Nottinghamshire 'keepers to have clocked up over 300 appearances.

Unlike Oates, Lilley was a very useful batsman, indeed the best specialist wicketkeeper batsman ever to play for Nottinghamshire. In times of crisis, as in 1930, he was often called upon to open the innings. In his first full season, he scored over 1,000 runs, the first Notts 'keeper to achieve this feat, repeating this in 1928 with a highly creditable Championship average of 28.83. On at least three other occasions he was to pass the 900-run mark in a season. Altogether he recorded 7 hundreds for the county, often rapid affairs, although he was capable of grafting out an innings if the occasion demanded. His 115 against Northamptonshire in 315 minutes in the penultimate game of 1929 virtually assured the county its Championship success.

He was equally consistent behind the stumps. For ten years, he claimed over 50 dismissals, on average about 69 per season; in 1926, his 80 dis-missals establishing a county record which lasted until 1991. His 30 stumpings in that season still remains unbeaten to the present day. He was the most successful 'keeper in the Championship in that year, and the second most successful in 1927 and 1935. His best performance in a match came in 1932, when he took nine catches against Somerset at Taunton, including six in one innings, equalling the county record. He finished his career as Nottinghamshire's second most successful 'keeper with 781 dismissals and still remains in third place today behind Oates and French.

Although being a highly useful run-getter, and having the experience of 'keeping to Larwood and Voce, taking 158 catches off the former, he was never apparently considered for an England place. He was also unfortunate when taking over as temporary captain in 1934 after Carr suffered a breakdown. Lilley led the side for seventeen games at a time when there was growing unease about the county's bowling tactics in the wake of the Bodyline series, and he captained the side in the controversial fixture against the Australians, which was to have severe repercussions for the county.

His decline in both batting and 'keeping in 1936 saw him replaced by Maxwell and Wheat, and he was to make only one appearance in 1937, when it was sadly reported in *Wisden* that 'Lilley excelled; but an injured thumb prevented him keeping wicket on the last day, and he did not play again.' He continued to play a number of games for Sir Julien Cahn's XI and, as with many of his former colleagues, he ended his days as a public house landlord.

Martin McIntyre
RHB & RF (round-arm), 1868-77

Born: 15 August 1847, Eastwood, Nottinghamshire

Died: 28 February 1885, Moor Green, Nottinghamshire

Batting

M	I	NO	Runs	HS
45	73	3	1145	88*
Ave	50	100	ct/st	
16.35	2	-	23	

Bowling

Runs	Wkts	Av	BB	5wI	10wM
1663	123	13.52	9-33	8	2

Best Performances

88* v. Surrey, The Oval, 1872
9-33 v. Surrey, The Oval, 1872

Martin was the youngest of three brothers from the Eastwood mining family of McIntyre, all of whom were to appear for the county. The eldest, Michael, appeared in only one game in 1864, whilst William, after a highly promising beginning, transferred his allegiance to Lancashire, enjoying considerable success for several years. Martin, like his elder brother William, was also a right-hand, fast round-arm bowler, making his first-class debut for the county in 1868, at the age of nineteen, and taking 5-33 against Yorkshire on his second appearance. The county at this time possessed a high-class bowling attack, which may have persuaded McIntyre to try his luck elsewhere.

In 1869 and 1870, he played his cricket in the USA, becoming the first player to score two centuries in an American season. He returned to appear in only three Nottinghamshire games in 1871, but then followed four years in which he was an ever-present in the side. His undoubted ability was reflected in his achievement as leading bowler in both 1872 and 1874, in an attack which boasted bowlers of the calibre of Wootton, the two Shaws and Morley. His greatest all-round performance came against Surrey at The Oval in 1872 when, coming in to bat with the score at 7-55, he struck an unbeaten 88, helping to add 147 for the eighth wicket with Richard Daft. He followed this with first innings figures of 9-33, seven clean-bowled and one caught and bowled, still the best figures by a Nottinghamshire bowler against Surrey. He returned match figures of 12-99 and scored a total of 115 runs for once out, the second

Nottinghamshire player after John Jackson to achieve the feat of ten wickets and a century in a match. This performance was all the more remarkable as McIntyre was a last-minute replacement for Alfred Shaw and had, prior to the match, been reprimanded for ill discipline. McIntyre did have a drink problem, which caused him to be left out of the side in 1876. On tour with W.G. Grace's side in Australia in 1873/74, W.G. later diplomatically wrote that 'the hospitality of our friends ... was too much for him and he sat up later than he should have'. It was probably why Daft remarked that 'if he had taken the trouble, he might have been 'one of the finest all-round men who ever played cricket'.

From 1872 to 1875, his fiery fast-bowling, sometimes peppered with wides and no-balls, and his hard-hitting produced a number of memorable individual performances, including 8-55 against Surrey in 1873, when he took the final five wickets in eleven balls for no runs. In the same year, he also returned figures of 8-18 for the North against the South at Lord's, then striking a 77 in the second innings. After a year's absence in 1876, he made only three further appearances for the county in the following year, seven of his nine wickets coming in one match. It was virtually the end of his first-class career, and he was to die of consumption at the early age of thirty-seven.

Frank Cyril Leonard Matthews
RHB & RF, 1920-27

Born: 15 August 1892, Willoughby-on-the
 Wolds, Nottinghamshire
Died: 11 January 1961, Nottingham

Batting

M	I	NO	Runs	HS
82	94	24	500	34
Ave	50	100	ct/st	
7.14	-	-	42	

Bowling

Runs	Wkts	Av	BB	5wI	10wM
5331	261	20.42	9-50	14	2

Best Performances
34 v. Cambridge University, Cambridge, 1925
9-50 v. Northamptonshire, Nottingham, 1923

Although Frank Matthews was with the county for eight years, he was to play only one full season, one which was to write him into the county's record books. His match figures of 17-89 achieved in that season are still the best recorded by a Nottinghamshire bowler in first-class cricket.

A local club cricketer and a professional for a Scottish club, he attracted attention with a number of performances whilst serving during the First World War. His debut season came in 1920 when he appeared in five county fixtures, finishing the season on a high note with 5-62 against Kent, claiming amongst his victims the great Frank Woolley for a duck. At twenty-eight years old, he was no youngster, but in the aftermath of the First World War, many counties with ageing sides were on the lookout for new faces. Matthews, 6ft tall with a good physique, appeared a good prospect, even if lacking experience of top-flight cricket and possessing a rather ungainly action. On his day he was extremely fast, bringing the ball down from a considerable height, thus proving a handful for many batsmen. He could also be expensive, Hendren once hitting him for 5 fours in an over in his debut season.

By 1922 he seemed to be making progress, claiming 37 wickets at a very reasonable average of 18.02. His great year was 1923, when he finished top of the county's bowling averages with 115 wickets at a cost of a mere 15.30 runs apiece,

an average that pushed him into fifth place in the national averages. He began with 6-52 against Middlesex at the end of May, but no one was prepared for his performances in the final two weeks of June, when, after taking 5-28 against Essex, he ran through the Northamptonshire side in both innings, generating great pace on a hard pitch to finish with match figures of 17-89, his 8-39 in the first innings being followed by 9-50 in the second. He bowled only 30 overs in the entire game, *Wisden* commenting that he was not on long enough to get fatigued. His tally for the final two weeks in June amounted to 47 wickets in five games. Even though four of these games were against the weaker sides in the Championship, it was still an impressive performance. *Wisden*'s comment was cautious: 'One would not yet go so far as to describe him as a first-rate fast bowler but he certainly proved himself a dangerous one.' These reservations proved correct, as Matthews was to show only glimpses of his 1923 form.

His last great performance came against Kent at Canterbury in 1924, when, 'bowling as he had never bowled before', he took 8-33, this including a spell of six wickets for one run. Only twice more was he to take five wickets in an innings for the county, whilst the emergence of a young fast bowler, Harold Larwood, further restricted his opportunities. He left the county in 1928, returning to play and coach cricket in Scotland.

Eric Alfred Meads
RHB & WK, 1939-53

Born: 17 August 1916, Carrington, Nottingham

Batting

M	I	NO	Runs	HS
205	240	90	1475	56*
Ave	50	100	ct/st	
9.83	2	-	364/83	

Bowling

Runs	Wkts	Av	BB	5wI	10wM
5	0	-	-	-	-

Best Performances
56* v. Worcestershire, Nottingham, 1948

In the county's team-sheet in the post-war era, it would have come as a considerable shock not to find the name of E.A. Meads in its familiar place at number eleven in the batting order. A diminutive cricketer, standing only 5ft 4in and weighing 8 ½st, he played for the City Schools before joining the staff in 1937. He played in every Second XI fixture in the two seasons before the war, making just one first-class appearance in the final month of 1939, when the regular 'keeper, Arthur Wheat, stood down. It was a successful debut against Hampshire at Trent Bridge, Meads claiming four catches and one stumping. He was clearly destined to take over from the forty-year-old Wheat, with county coach Jimmy Iremonger going so far as to state that he would play for his country. Although serving in the RAF, Meads continued to play cricket for the county throughout the war, assisted by the county's determination to maintain fixtures at this time. In a fixture against a Services XI he claimed six victims in an innings, four of them being stumped, underlining the view that he was especially brilliant on the leg-

side. Commencing as the county's wicketkeeper in 1946, he was to play in 106 consecutive fixtures, before being rested for one game late in 1949 to give an opportunity to his deputy, Eddie Rowe. It was the longest consecutive run of appearances by a Notts 'keeper until surpassed by Geoff Millman in the early 1960s.

He was rarely out of the side, being hardly ever troubled by injury, missing only eight Championship games after the war until being replaced by Rowe in 1953, excluding 1946, he was to make over fifty dismissals every season; his best season being 1948 when his total of 74 dismissals was the highest by any 'keeper in the country. His highest number in a match was seven victims against Kent in 1949 and he shared the then Notts record of six in an innings (since beaten by Noon in 1999) achieving this on two occasions. His batting can only be described as undistinguished, although he did manage 2 fifties, a top score of 56* in 1948 and an initial unbeaten fifty in 1946, when he took part in a tenth wicket unbroken partnership of 110 with Freddie Stocks against Worcestershire – allowing Stocks to reach his hundred and assisting Notts to an innings victory. In 1953 he appeared in every fixture up to his benefit game against Derbyshire but the following game proved to be his last. After a stint in the Second XI, he retired in 1954.

Geoffrey Millman
RHB & WK, 1957-65

Born: 2 October 1934, Bedford

Batting

M	I	NO	Runs	HS
257	440	48	7410	131*
4	3	0	24	14

Ave	50	100	ct/st
18.90	25	3	517/82
8.00	-	-	5/1

Bowling

Runs	Wkts	Av	BB	5wl	10wM
32	0	-	-	-	-

Best Performances
131* v. Kent, Nottingham, 1960
14 v. Somerset, Taunton, 1964

Although Geoff Millman left the county at the relatively early age of thirty-one, he gave good service at a time when Nottinghamshire was experiencing one of the most unrewarding periods in its long history. He was never omitted from the side after making his debut in 1957, appearing in 240 out of a possible 252 Championship fixtures. Millman had attracted attention whilst 'keeping for Bedfordshire, for whom he made his debut at the age of nineteen and then for the Combined Services whilst undertaking his National Service with the RAF. Notts were on the lookout for a wicketkeeper batsman of high quality and the twenty-two-year-old Millman appeared to fill the bill perfectly.

After an unfortunate start, with Millman contracting mumps after only four games, he enjoyed his first season with the county; taking full advantage of an attack which comprised Dooland, Goonesena and Smales, he claimed 22 stumpings out of his total of 60 victims. It was a standard he was to maintain consistently throughout his Nottinghamshire career. In nine consecutive seasons he recorded a minimum of fifty victims each year, a record bettered only by Ben Lilley. His most productive season behind the stumps came in 1961 when his total of 85 in Nottinghamshire matches surpassed Lilley's record of 81 in 1926. Considering the non-penetrative nature of the county attack by this time, it was an impressive record, which was to win him selection for the MCC tour to India in 1961/62.

Millman had been tipped as a future England wicketkeeper from the early days of his career with his neat, calm work behind the stumps. He had also progressed as a sound, competent batsman, who had moved up the order to open the innings by 1960, having completed 1,000 runs in the previous season. In 1961 his aggregate of 1,306 was the highest by any Nottinghamshire 'keeper, he and Ben Lilley being the only two wicketkeepers to reach this target on two occasions for the county. He scored 3 hundreds for the county, his highest innings being an unbeaten 131* against Kent in 1960.

Millman went out to India and Pakistan in 1960/61 as J.T. Murray's deputy but forced his way into the Test side for the last four Tests of the tour, retaining his place for a further two against Pakistan in England in the 1962 season. He was the first Nottinghamshire 'keeper to play for England since Mordecai Sherwin way back in 1888. For the final three seasons with the county, Millman also took on the burden of captaincy, Nottinghamshire's fourth captain in as many years, retaining it until he chose to retire at the end of the 1965 season. To his credit as captain he had played in every Championship, making 143 consecutive appearances, only three short of George Heane's record. His best performances for the county were six dismissals in an innings, which equalled the county record, and nine dismissals in a match.

Frederick Morley

LHB & LF, 1872-83

Born: 16 December 1850, Sutton-in-Ashfield, Nottinghamshire

Died: 28 September 1884, Sutton-in-Ashfield, Nottinghamshire

Batting

M	I	NO	Runs	HS
113	159	32	696	31
Ave	50	100	ct/st	
5.48	-	-	54	

Bowling

Runs	Wkts	Av	BB	5wI	10wM
8168	666	12.26	8-26	64	19

Best Performances

Batting: 31 v. Kent, Canterbury, 1877
Bowling: 8-26 v. Kent, Town Malling, 1878

Frederick Morley was yet another bowler of the highest quality who appeared for Nottinghamshire in the nineteenth century. A left-arm fast bowler but an indifferent batsman and fielder, he combined exceptional accuracy with the ability to move the ball from leg across the batsman's body, resulting in many catches to slip and point. Above all he was a match-winner. Amiable, easy-going, modest and rarely ruffled, Richard Daft wrote that 'Fewer cricketers had fewer enemies and more friends than Fred Morley.'

Although never taking a hat-trick or more than eight wickets in an innings, his wicket taking can only be described as phenomenal. In the ten full seasons of cricket in which he played, he was to achieve a hundred or more wickets on seven occasions. His great year was 1878 when he took 197 wickets in all games and became the first Nottinghamshire bowler to take over a hundred in a season in county matches alone. He recorded five or more wickets in an innings in twelve of his fifteen games and ten or more wickets in a match on five occasions, both county records at that time, also heading the county's averages as he did in 1877 and 1879. He formed a lethal combination with Alfred Shaw, the pair running through side with consummate ease in the late 1870s. They bowled unchanged throughout a match on six occasions for the county, their most notable achievements being the dismissal of the Australians for 63 and 76 and Kent for 36 and 50; Morley recording his best match figures of 15-35 and his best innings

analysis, 8-26 in the latter fixture. His first innings figure of 7-9 marked the second of three occasions when he was to claim seven wickets in an innings for under ten runs for Nottinghamshire, his best being in 1877 when he took 7-7 against Derbyshire (16 all out) at Trent Bridge. He was also to claim 7-9 against Surrey at The Oval in 1880.

Morley was also highly successful for other sides. In 1877 on a helpful pitch, for MCC he returned figures of 7-6 and 6-8 against Oxford University, who were dismissed for 12 and 35. Morley's match figures of 13-14 is still the most economical thirteen-wicket analysis in first-class cricket. He was selected for the first Test to be played in England in 1880, taking 5-56 on his debut at The Oval and played in three Tests in Australia in 1882/83 after sustaining a broken rib on the journey out, which proved a major handicap throughout the tour. Whether the injury exacerbated his increasingly poor health, which had affected him prior to the tour, is debatable but after a few appearances in the early part of 1883 he was forced to stand down and he died of dropsy the following year aged thirty-three. Many of the county records he achieved still stand to this day. Six of the current counties all registered their lowest totals against Nottinghamshire during Morley's short but outstanding bowling career, a fitting legacy for one of the county's greatest bowlers.

Thomas William Oates
RHB & WK, 1897-1925

Born: 9 August 1875, Eastwood, Nottinghamshire
Died: 18 June 1949, Eastwood, Nottinghamshire

Batting

M	I	NO	Runs	HS
420	559	106	5884	88
Ave	50	100	ct/st	
12.98	15	-	733/224	

Bowling

Runs	Wkts	Av	BB	5wI	10wM
20	0	-	-	-	-

Best Performances
Batting: 88 v. Kent, Nottingham, 1920

Tom Oates was one of the great servants of Nottinghamshire CCC, an enthusiastic but undemonstrative wicketkeeper who over twenty-eight seasons played practically all his first-class cricket for the county. Oates was a local cricketer whose potential as a wicketkeeper was recognised when in 1897 he was one of five young players to be chosen for the county's ground staff; this in itself was a new venture by the club to unearth fresh talent. Oates made his debut towards the end of the season against Gloucestershire, an interesting introduction to Championship cricket, as he watched at close hand W.G. Grace score 131. At twenty-two years of age he was second in line after the current 'keeper, Arthur Pike, but the latter's illness gave him his chance in 1899. Frustratingly Oates was then forced to take second place to Carlin towards the end of the season, the latter proving to be the better batsman of the two. Only with Carlin's retirement at the end of 1901 did Oates establish himself as the county's regular 'keeper, maintaining his high standards until his retirement twenty-four years later.

In that time he established new county wicketkeeping records. In 1906 he claimed 59 dismissals behind the stumps, beating Sherwin's tally of 50 in 1887. He was to record over fifty dismissals for the county on six further occasions; in 1922 and 1923 he claimed 65 victims, a record later overtaken by Ben Lilley in 1926. His final total for

Nottinghamshire was 957, still a county record. He became the first Nottinghamshire 'keeper to claim six victims in an innings, firstly against Middlesex at Trent Bridge in 1906 and again against Leicestershire the following year at Leicester. In the Middlesex game, he stumped one and caught nine in the match, his aggregate of ten being a new county record, beating Sherwin's eight victims in 1889. Oates also claimed eight dismissals in a match on two other occasions.

He was capable of making useful runs down the order, his highest innings being 88 against Kent in 1920, assisting in creating a new county record of 195 for the eighth wicket with Payton, a record that stood until 1935. When he eventually retired in 1925, aged 49 years 304 days, the oldest 'keeper to have appeared for the county, he had at that stage made the second highest number of appearances for the county after John Gunn's 489. His 420 appearances is still the fourth highest number for Nottinghamshire. He remained in the game as a first-class umpire, standing in five Tests, and then became the county scorer.

William Oscroft

RHB & RF (round-arm), 1864-82

Born: 16 December 1843, Arnold, Nottinghamshire
Died: 10 October 1905, Nottingham

Batting

M	I	NO	Runs	HS
167	281	14	5237	140
Ave	50	100	ct/st	
19.61	20	2	130/1	

Bowling

Runs	Wkts	Av	BB	5wI	10wM
1127	59	19.10	5-34	2	-

Best Performances
Batting: 140 v. Kent, Canterbury, 1879
Bowling: 5-34 v. Yorkshire, Nottingham, 1876

William (pictured seated, second from right) Oscroft's obituary in *Wisden* commented that 'never, perhaps, did a young batsman make a more brilliant first appearance'. The performance referred to was at Lord's in 1864 when opening the batting for the Colts of England against the MCC, he scored 51 and 76 against two of the leading bowlers in England, George Wootton and James Grundy, both Nottinghamshire men, on a pitch traditionally helpful to bowlers. Within a month he was to make his Nottinghamshire debut against Kent, many hoping that he would prove a worthy successor to George Parr.

Oscroft came from a cricketing family, his uncle having played for the Nottingham Club and his brother subsequently appearing for Nottinghamshire. Although initially an all-rounder, he was to give up his fast round-arm bowling to concentrate on his batting, although remaining a useful change bowler. He was an attractive, attacking batsman, with a penchant for leg-side shots. Richard Daft described him as 'one of the finest leg-hitters we ever saw and one of the hardest'. Daft's further remark that 'his hitting all round was a treat ... whenever he was well set', gives a clue to Oscroft's subsequent erratic form.

Oscroft's 1865 form seemed to justify all the earlier expectations of his talent. He scored the sole Nottinghamshire century of the season, 107 against Sussex at Hove, also sharing a first-wicket county record partnership against Cambridgeshire of 146. He became the first batsman to carry his bat for the county when he made an unbeaten 53* out of 94 against Surrey.

At twenty-one years of age he headed both the Nottinghamshire and the national averages with what was then a phenomenal average of 51.44. Sadly he was not to enjoy a similar season for the remainder of his seventeen-year career with the Nottinghamshire club.

By 1868 he had dropped down the order and after his dismissal first ball in both innings against Surrey he was left out of the side for the remainder of the season. He experienced another disastrous season in 1871, when he averaged only 5.60, finishing below J.C. Shaw, arguably the county's worst-ever batsman, in the averages. Otherwise he remained an automatic choice for the county until ill health forced his retirement in 1882 at the age of thirty-eight. He enjoyed an Indian summer in 1879 when he was to average 32.31, having scored 614 runs in his 21 appearances. This included the second century of his career, 140 against Kent, adding 192 for the second wicket with Selby, who was at that time the highest partnership for any wicket for the county.

Apart from his career with Nottinghamshire, he was a regular member of the All England XI, taking over the reins of secretary from George Parr in 1876 in the remaining few years of its existence. He appeared for the Players on fifteen occasions and also for other representative elevens and participated in two overseas tours, with W.G. Grace's team to Australia in 1873/74 and with Richard Daft's side to North America in 1879.

Born: 22 May 1826, Radcliffe-on-Trent,
Nottinghamshire
Died: 23 June 1891, Radcliffe-on-Trent,
Nottinghamshire

Batting

M	I	NO	Runs	HS
54	89	9	1804	130
Ave	**50**	**100**	**ct/st**	
22.55	6	1	33	

Best Performances
130 v. Surrey, The Oval, 1859

Until 1976 when gales blew it down, an elm tree on Bridgford Road, known as Parr's tree, marked the spot when George Parr (centre of picture) allegedly struck many of his renowned hits to leg. Parr, known as the 'Lion of the North' was accepted throughout the 1850s as the premier professional batsman in England. In addition he was to carry on the work of the other great Nottinghamshire cricketing pioneer, William Clarke, by taking over the organisation of the All England XI after Clarke's death in 1856, as well as becoming captain of the Nottingham-shire side until his retirement in 1870. In terms of results he still remains the most successful Nottinghamshire captain, leading the team to 22 victories in 36 games. He was also to captain the first touring side to visit America and Canada in 1859 and the second side to visit Australia in 1863/64.

Parr, one of three brothers to play for Nottinghamshire, made his first appearance for the county in 1845 after impressing William Clarke the previous year in an appearance for the Players of Notts. Like many future great players, Parr made his mark on the game with the evolution of a new batting technique. The development of round-arm bowling, especially of the faster kind, often bowled round the wicket, increased the number of deliveries on or outside the leg stump. Parr evolved the leg sweep to hit anything outside the leg stump as well as becoming highly effective with the pull shot. Most commentators of the day accepted that he was the greatest leg-hitter ever seen. He was also one of the modern school of batsmen who defied tradition by refusing to stand in his crease to play the ball. William Caffyn remarked that 'he played a different game to anyone who had preceded him, using his feet and going out to drive straight balls far more than anyone else'. Lillywhite used to complain when Parr advanced down the wicket to drive an over pitched ball that this was 'not cricket'. Richard Daft also supports the view that he was not simply a leg hitter, writing in *Kings of Cricket* that 'those who think he could only hit to leg are vastly mistaken, as he could cut and drive almost equally well'.

With the establishment of the All England XI by Clarke, there was a dearth of county games during the 1840s and '50s when Parr was at the height of his powers, although he was an automatic choice for the county, appearing in twenty-two out of the twenty-four Nottingham-shire games played prior to 1860. His first innings of over fifty for the county came in 1848 when he scored 52 against Sussex at Hove. Four more followed in this period, culminating in his 130 against Surrey at The Oval in 1859; batting for 330 minutes, he recorded the first hundred for the county. *Wisden* commented that 'all who witnessed that display being unanimous in awarding it the high praise of being one of the most perfectly played innings they had ever seen'. In the context of the times this was an outstanding achievement; in those 22 games only 15 half-centuries were scored, Parr making five of them and also playing the only three-figure innings. In his final eleven seasons for Notts he was to reach fifty on only one further occasion, his appearances becoming more intermittent through injury and illness.

George Parr, 'the Lion of the North', the greatest professional batsman of his day.

Richard Daft and George Parr.

He was to be an automatic choice for all the major representative matches until the mid-1860s, making 21 appearances for the Players, 38 for the North and 77 for various England XIs, reaching over fifty in these games on 22 occasions. His consistency in the big games is reflected in his final averages: 25.31 for the Players and 20.36 for England as opposed to 22.69 for Nottinghamshire.

With such an excellent batting record, it is no surprise that he was to play a prominent part in the AEE during the whole of his cricket career, taking over the organisation and captaincy of the AEE after Clarke's death in 1856. He was to appear in an estimated 357 Odds matches between 1847 and 1871, hitting 3 centuries and 26 fifties. Of the forty-seven important and first-class matches played by the AEE, Parr appeared in thirty-eight; it was by far the most of any player, being the only batsman to score over 1,000 runs, his final tally being 1416 at an average of 23.21.

A powerful and influential man in the game, Parr attracted both loyal friends and critical ene-mies. He was accused, by Lillywhite amongst others, of being bad-tempered, jealous and conceited. Even Richard Daft was to assert that his players stood in awe of him, for Parr 'was always rather a queer-tempered man', although Daft also described him as a 'man under whose banner I am proud to have fought. Another asserted 'a more honest and straight cricketer never took hold of a bat'. He was involved in a longstanding feud concerning umpires and financial matters with the Surrey club from 1861; Parr refused to appear at The Oval after this date and persuaded others not to play there or against Surrey. Some alleged that Parr deliberately arranged AEE fixtures to coincide with the showpieces at Lord's and The Oval, thus reducing their importance. Only in his final first-class appearance in 1870 did he decide to play against Surrey at Trent Bridge. He retired to Radcliffe-on-Trent, living a quiet life, although he remained the nominal secretary of the AEE until 1875, rarely watching any cricket at Trent Bridge until his death in 1891, aged sixty-five.

Wilfred Richard Daniel Payton
RHB, 1905-31

Born: 13 February 1882, Stapleford,
   Nottinghamshire
Died: 2 May 1943, Beeston Fields,
   Nottinghamshire

Batting

M	I	NO	Runs	HS
489	766	126	22079	169
Ave	50	100	ct/st	
34.49	113	39	144	

Bowling

Runs	Wkts	Av	BB	5wI	10wM
68	1	68.00	1-18	-	-

Best Performances
169 v. Lancashire, Nottingham, 1929
1-18 v. Northamptonshire, Northampton, 1922

Payton made his county debut in 1905 at the age of twenty-four and from 1906 remained a permanent member of the side until his retirement from the game twenty-five years later. In that time he amassed a total of 489 appearances, a number surpassed only by George Gunn, including two sequences of 126 consecutive games between 1907 and 1913, and 125 between 1914 and 1923. He was the only Notts player to have achieved over a hundred consecutive appearances on two occasions. Payton played only two other first-class games in his lengthy career, never being selected for the Players or a Test trial. To those who witnessed his early years, this would have come as something of a surprise, for accounts of the day described him as a batsman of the future, possessing a sound defence, a wide range of strokes and an orthodox style. His century against the West Indian tourists in his first full season and a highly impressive unbeaten 149 against Surrey at The Oval the following year in 170 minutes (which included 126 runs before lunch on the third day) appeared to confirm this view.

His contribution to the Championship success of 1907 also kept him in the public eye. Yet although playing a number of admirable innings, he failed to achieve 1,000 runs in a season until 1921, his twelfth in the first-class game. From then onwards he remained one of the county's most consistent and reliable batsmen, reaching over 1,000 runs in his next eight seasons whilst in his forties. These were his most productive years, 1926 bringing him 1,864 runs, averaging 47 an innings, in a year when he missed a number of games through illness. From 1925 to 1929 he was to average over forty a season, in part the consequence of his ability to remain unbeaten, with 16 per cent of his innings falling into this category. Usually going in at number five, his experience and sound defence, especially his back play on rain-affected pitches enabled him on many occasions to stem the loss of early wickets. It was said that the more desperate the situation, the better he played.

He was a key member of the Championship-winning side of 1929, sharing with George Gunn the distinction of having also appeared in the victorious 1907 Championship XI. In 1929, aged forty-seven, he made the highest score of his career, a faultless and almost inevitably unbeaten 169 against Lancashire. Although still playing well in 1930, he was left out of the side, along with George Gunn, in the interests of bringing along younger players but injuries sustained by key players earned a final recall to the side for four games in 1931. At 49 years 168 days he is the seventh oldest player to have appeared for Nottinghamshire and on his retirement only George and John Gunn had scored more runs for the county.

Robert Andrew Pick

LHB and RFM, 1983-1997

Born: 19 November 1963, Nottingham

Batting

M	I	NO	Runs	HS
186	197	52	2205	65*
194	78	42	608	58*
Ave	50	100	ct/st	
15.21	5	-	48	
16.88	1	-	38	

Bowling

Runs	Wkts	Av	BB	5wI	10wM
15640	454	34.44	7-128	13	2
7422	226	32.84	5-22	2	-

Best Performances

65* v. Northamptonshire, Nottingham, 1994
58* v. Essex, Nottingham, 1995
7-128 v. Leicestershire, Leicester, 1990
5-22 v. Gloucestershire, Bristol, 1987

The son of a well-known local cricketer, Andy Pick soon made his mark in schoolboy cricket, appearing in the England Schools Cricket Association Under-19 team in 1982, being described as the quickest bowler in the side. By this time he had also been drafted into the Nottinghamshire Second XI, making an appearance when only sixteen years old. His potential as a young fast bowler was recognised when he was selected for all three 'Tests' against the Young Australians in 1983.

Over the next four seasons he worked his way gradually into the First XI, at a time when the county was fielding one of its strongest bowling attacks. In only his second season he returned match figures of 10-58 in the opening match of the season against Oxford University, and after taking 50 wickets in 1986 he was capped in Nottinghamshire's Championship winning year. His most memorable match to date was the NatWest semi-final against Gloucestershire at Bristol when his 5-22, including three of the first four batsmen, made him Man of the Match and saw Nottinghamshire into their victorious final at Lord's, in which he removed the dangerous top-scorer Larkins. This was a limited overs competition in which he was to excel, his 50 wickets at the very economical 23.72 apiece being the highest number by a Nottinghamshire bowler.

In 1995 he again returned excellent figures of 5-23 against Scotland, which included Nottinghamshire's first hat-trick in NatWest Trophy games, all lbw. He was unfortunate that with the retirement of both Rice and Hadlee in 1987, injuries were to limit his Championship appearances to only eleven in the next two sea-sons at a time when he should have been approaching his peak. In a make-or-break season in 1990, although still troubled by injury, he enjoyed his best year to date, taking 51 wickets and returning a career-best 7-128 against Leicestershire, earning him his second ten wickets in a match. Of greater importance he was selected for the England A tour to Pakistan and Sri Lanka, where he was to play the best cricket of his career. He played in all three Unofficial 'Tests' and headed the tour averages, taking 21 wickets at a cost of 17 apiece, being the only bowler to take five wickets in an innings. He followed this with his most successful domestic season, taking 65 wickets and missing only one Championship game, the only season in which he was to appear in over twenty games. This earned him a further England A tour, this time to the West Indies, where he played in two of the three Unofficial Tests with reasonable success.

Unfortunately, injuries again surfaced in 1992 and until he was released by the county in 1997 he experienced only two more full seasons, in both of which he claimed over fifty wickets; in 1994 he averaged fewer than thirty for the only time in his county career. He was recently appointed as an ECB coach to the North-East and is also involved with the England Under-17 and Under-19 sides.

Paul Raymond Pollard
LHB & RM, 1987-98

Born: 24 September 1968, Nottingham

Batting

M	I	NO	Runs	HS
157	275	20	8347	180
145	134	13	3962	132*

Ave	50	100	ct/st
32.73	40	13	148
32.74	22	4	55

Bowling

Runs	Wkts	Av	BB	5wI	10wM
268	4	67.00	2-79	-	-
9	0	-	-	-	-

Best Performances

180 v. Derbyshire, Nottingham, 1993
132 v. Somerset, Nottingham, 1995*
2-79 v. Gloucestershire, Bristol, 1993

Taken on at Trent Bridge through a YTS scheme, Paul Pollard soon showed that he possessed the necessary talent to pursue a worthwhile first-class career. By 1987, after a prolific season in the Second XI, he made his first-class debut aged 18 years 311 days against Derbyshire, making a bright start against Holding and Malcolm and sharing an opening stand of 72 in 96 minutes.

Opportunities were limited in his early years, with Broad and Robinson opening, but Pollard, a more than useful stand-in, showed his ability to occupy the crease when he batted for 471 minutes in achieving his maiden hundred, 142 against Kent in 1988. It was, however, his attacking qualities which were more representative of his approach, these coming to the fore in 1989, when he enjoyed a record-breaking season. In one marvellous week he amassed 544 runs, a total which included three hundreds, including two against Kent. The first of these marked his initial hundred in limited overs cricket, scored in only 102 balls, making him the youngest Notts batsman to score a century in the Sunday League. A highest Championship score of 131 was followed by 153 in 180 minutes against Cambridge University. During this purple patch, Pollard recorded a unique achievement in English cricket, together with Robinson, putting together two opening partnerships of 222 and 282 against Kent in the Championship fixture. Coincidentally, Notts

also met Kent in a Benson & Hedges fixture in the same week, Pollard hitting 77 in 100 balls, this time sharing an opening stand of 141 with Broad. By the end of the season he had become the youngest Nottinghamshire batsman to have reached 1,000 runs in a season and had made the highest score, an unbeaten 123 against Surrey, by a Notts batsman in the Sunday League.

Still only twenty years old, he made only five appearances in 1990 with Broad and Robinson being fully available, but he then became a regular member of the side for the following four seasons. In two of those years he reached 1,000 runs, his best season being 1993, when he topped the county's averages with 1,463 runs at an impressive average of 50.44 and scored a career-best 180 against Derbyshire. It was a game in which he again featured in two century opening partnerships, this time 291 and 150 with Dessaur. Another highlight was a century before lunch on the first day. He was the fifth Nottinghamshire batsman to achieve this, his hundred against Lancashire coming off 104 balls against an attack including Wasim Akram and Philip de Freitas. He also adopted a positive approach in limited overs cricket, both as an opening batsman and in the middle order, in 1995 striking 7 consecutive fifties. His final average of 32.74 in these games remains amongst the best for the county.

Less publicised was his close catching ability, his best year being 1993 when he held 25 catches. Perhaps disillusioned that his very satisfactory record as a specialist opener had not been rewarded by a permanent place in the side, he opted to continue his career with Worcestershire after 1998.

Born: 13 March 1921, Forest Town, Mansfield, Nottinghamshire
Died: 11 February 1996, Newark, Nottinghamshire

Batting

M	I	NO	Runs	HS
366	615	40	18658	222*
Ave	50	100	ct/st	
32.49	120	24	215/5	

Bowling

Runs	Wkts	Av	BB	5wl	10wM
259	2	129.50	1-11	-	-

Best Performances
222* v. Indians, Nottingham, 1952
1-11 v. Sussex, Nottingham, 1959

A highly talented young sportsman, Cyril Poole was the youngest footballer (aged fifteen) to appear in Mansfield Town's colours, later going on to play for Gillingham and Wolves. He was equally precocious at cricket, at the age of twenty scoring an unbeaten 101 on his first appearance for the county against the RAF in 1941, putting on 208 for the first wicket in 75 minutes with another promising young batsman, Reg Simpson. Service in the Army as a physical training instructor delayed his first-class debut until the age of twenty-seven, when he fulfilled his early promise with an unbeaten 143 against Sussex in only his seventh first-class innings. He gained a permanent place in the side in the following season, establishing his credentials as a highly attractive forcing bat and an outstanding fielder in the deep. Evidence of this came against Leicestershire at Trent Bridge, when with Simpson he added 251 for the second wicket in only 97 minutes, Poole reaching three figures in 60 minutes. It was the fastest century of the 1949 season. At a time when the only chance of a victory at Trent Bridge was to chase a target, Poole was a major asset to the side as a hard-hitting, aggressive middle-order batsman. Although a risk-taker, Poole only failed to reach the target of 1,000 runs once between 1949 and 1961.

However, the very nature of his play – his desire to play strokes and attack the bowling – did lead to spells of inconsistency. He was not a batsman to occupy the crease for long periods of play, one exception being his career-best unbeaten 222* against the Indians which took an uncharacteristic 450 minutes. Three weeks later he was to achieve his only other first-class double-century, a more typical Poole innings, when against Jackson and Gladwin at Ilkeston, he struck 219 out of 337 including 3 sixes and 33 fours, almost 65.5 per cent of his side's runs. He surpassed this feat in 1960 at Bristol, hitting 87 out of a Notts total of 121, 71.95 per cent of the total and the best by a Nottinghamshire batsman until beaten by Clive Rice in 1981. At the end of his career he particularly enjoyed batting against the formidable Surrey attack, scoring 109, which included 3 sixes and 15 fours, at Trent Bridge in 1960, and in the return match on a rain-affected pitch top-scoring in both innings, hitting 64 in 57 minutes in the first innings, striking 3 sixes and 5 fours. The last of his 24 hundreds came the following year when, aged forty, he reached three figures in 120 minutes at The Oval, his 126 containing 4 sixes and 13 fours.

After an excellent season in 1951, when he stood fourth in the national averages, he secured a place in the MCC touring party to India. Sustaining a broken finger, he missed the first ten games of the tour, but then appeared in his sole three Tests, making 55 and 69* in his Test debut at Eden Gardens. At his best Poole was one of the most attractive, enterprising and dangerous left-hand batsmen in the 1950s; he was a natural striker of the ball, who was never afraid to take on any bowling attack in the country.

Born: 24 February 1951, Retford, Nottinghamshire

Batting

M	I	NO	Runs	HS
393	669	67	23069	237
403	383	53	10839	149*

Ave	50	100	ct/st
38.32	134	40	290
32.84	69	6	81

Bowling

Runs	Wkts	Av	BB	5wl	10wM
376	12	31.33	3-15	-	-
37	-	-	-	-	-

Best Performances
237 v. Derbyshire, Nottingham, 1988
149 v. Devon, Torquay, 1988*
3-15 v. MCC, Lord's, 1982

Without doubt, Derek Randall was the most popular cricketer to have appeared for the county since the Second World War, rivalling the affection for George Gunn in earlier decades. He made an impressive first-class debut at the Newark Ground against Essex in 1972, with a typical innings of 78, striking 5 sixes and 4 fours. His positive approach to batting, coupled with his outstanding ability at cover, soon won him a place in 1973 in the Young England XI against the West Indies, a game in which he top-scored. In 1973 he achieved his maiden first-class hundred, a 'splendid speedy' affair, being capped by his county and being discussed, rather prematurely, as a possible for the tour to West Indies in 1973/74. He gained his first representative honours in 1976, appearing in two one-day international fixtures against the West Indies, where his ability against their renowned fast bowling attack led to him being named Man of the Series. This performance, plus two excellent seasons of attacking cricket with the bat and outstanding performances in the field for Nottinghamshire (both of which yielded over 1,000 runs), earned him a place in the touring party to India and Australia. It was the beginning of a chequered Test career which was to earn Randall 47 caps, seven hundreds and 2470 runs between 1977 and 1984, all records for a Nottinghamshire player.

He captured the imagination of all cricket lovers with his 174 against Australia in the Centenary Test at Melbourne in 1976-77, his innings winning him the Man of the Match award. It encapsulated all the ingredients of his batting style, which came to infuriate so many bowlers; on this occasion, the ferocious Dennis Lillee, who was to call him, 'this bloody little pain in the arse'. Constantly fidgeting, tugging at his cap, touching his pads, talking to himself, doffing his cap to a Lillee bouncer, and playing a wide range of improvised strokes, he showed great courage by continuing after being struck on the temple by Lillee.

Some consider his 150 at Sydney in 1978-79 as the greater Test innings within the context of the match and series. With England one up in the series, Australia took a first innings lead of 142, Randall on a pair, came in first wicket down after Boycott went first ball to play the longest innings of his life, occupying the crease for 9 hours 49 minutes in a temperature of 105 degrees. His century in 411 minutes was the slowest at that time in Ashes Tests. It won him the Player of the Match award and was a major factor in England's victory and the retention of the Ashes. Yet he was to experience a patchy

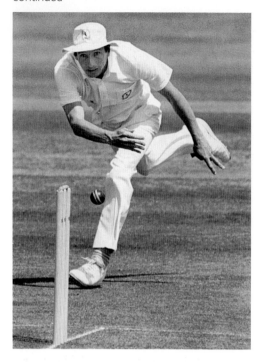

A fielder of the highest class, Derek Randall represents all that is good about the game of cricket.

Reaching 1,000 runs on eleven occasions, this figure being limited by representative calls and injuries in at least four other seasons, he enjoyed his best-ever season in 1985, being chosen as Championship player of the year after scoring 2,151 runs. Simon Hughes' comment that Randall was forever walking the tightrope between triumph and calamity was fully borne out in the NatWest final against Essex, when he brought Notts to the verge of a highly unbelievable victory, hitting 16 runs off Derek Pringle's final over, only to be caught off the final ball with just two runs required. In 1988 he hit the highest innings of his career, 237 against Derbyshire, the last of his three double-centuries.

His achievements place him amongst the Nottinghamshire greats. He had achieved over 20,000 Championship runs, 40 centuries and the unique county record of a double-century and a hundred in the same match, 209 and 146 against Middlesex at Trent Bridge in 1979. He also managed a century before lunch against Leicestershire in 1979. Only five players have taken more catches for the county. In 1991, aged forty, he finished top of the county's batting averages for the sixth time and played a significant part in the winning of the Sunday League, being involved in three century opening stands and never failing to reach double figures in sixteen appearances. At the end of 1992 only two other players had scored more runs in limited-overs cricket in England.

Test career, long runs in the side being followed by lengthy periods of omission. One newspaper writer went so far as to suggest that when England did badly, the Selectors' first decision was to drop Randall. Perhaps Randall was too accommodating, always being prepared to bat in any position if asked.

His second run in the England side was brought to an end after he was tried as an opener in Australia in 1979/80 in a side containing others more suited to the task. As a middle-order batsman he topped the Test averages in Australia in 1982/83 and finishing second in the 1983/84 tour of New Zealand and Pakistan. Many writers and spectators felt he had been sacrificed in what was to be his final Test appearance when asked to bat at three against the West Indies in 1984, with Gower and Lamb dropping down the order against the hostile West Indian attack. Coming to the wicket early in both innings, he made nought and one. It was a brutal end to his Test career.

He continued his county career for another eight years, his twenty-one playing seasons as a capped player being a county record. During that time the county won the three limited-overs competitions and the Championship twice.

After a long and distinguished career with the county, his last season proved to be a miserable affair. The manager's decision to 'concentrate on youth policy' meant that Randall appeared in the first five Championship games as an opener and a handful of limited overs games. It says much of the character of the man that he never complained. In his autobiography *Rags* his father, answering the point that everything was a joke with Derek, replied, 'Underneath he's serious. He cares desperately about cricket and Nottingham-shire cricket in particular.' His greatest gift was to share his love and enjoyment of the game with all those who were privileged to watch him bat and field.

Christopher Mark Wells Read
RHB & WKT, 1998-

Born: 10 August 1978, Paignton, Devon

Batting

M	I	NO	Runs	HS
78	126	20	2934	160
97	78	17	1329	69

Ave	50	100	ct/st
27.67	15	2	233/7
21.78	-	3	108/24

Bowling

Runs	Wkts	Av	BB	5wI	10wM
25	0	-	-	-	-

Best Performances
160 v. Warwickshire, Nottingham, 1999
69 v. Warwickshire, Birmingham, 2002

Even a cursory glance at Chris Read's cricket curriculum vitae suggests an England wicket-keeper in the making. An early burgeoning talent earned him a place in the Minor Counties Championship side, Devon, for three years and at sixteen for the Minor Counties in the NatWest Trophy. At the same time he was progressing through the various Under-17, Under-18 and Under-19 representative elevens, joining Gloucestershire in 1997. Without appearing in a single first-class match, he was selected for the England A tour to Kenya and Sri Lanka in the following winter, where he made his first-class debut and appeared in two of the unofficial Tests against Sri Lanka. With no immediate prospect of playing in the Gloucestershire XI with Jack Russell 'keeping, Read opted for Nottinghamshire as understudy for Wayne Noon. His chance came quickly; the unfortunate Noon broke a finger in only the fourth Championship game, which was to effectively end his first-class career with the county, with Read appearing in 75 of the next 78 Championship matches. His three missed games were the consequence of being called up by the England Selectors for the First Test against New Zealand in 1999.

At 20 years and 325 days, he was the youngest wicketkeeper to play for England in the twentieth century. He claimed eight wickets on his Test debut, and six in the second innings. It was a record for a debutant and *Wisden* was later to comment that 'he had shown enough grit to suggest he could yet become a pearl'. Grit he certainly showed in England's second innings at Lord's, when only his and Caddick's determined resistance prevented a humiliating innings defeat. Although subsequently selected for the England tour to South Africa and Zimbabwe in the winter as Stewart's understudy, he has since been ignored by the Selectors, although he did take part in the England A tour to West Indies in 2001/02.

However, his 68 victims in 2002, the most by any 'keeper in the country and including eight in a match against Essex at Trent Bridge, has again brought him into favour, with selection for the Australian Academy in the winter. This experience, added to that gained by 'keeping to Stuart McGill, should keep him well in contention for a return to the England side in the immediate future. In addition, his batting performances may also give him an edge. He had already demonstrated his batting ability when he recorded his maiden hundred, a highly impressive 160 against Warwickshire in 1999 which took only 208 balls and included 24 fours, 106 runs being scored between lunch and tea. He has now added consistency to his batting, averaging over thirty in both 2001 and 2002 and scoring his second hundred (127) in 2002.

Clive Edward Butler Rice
RHB & RFM, 1975-87

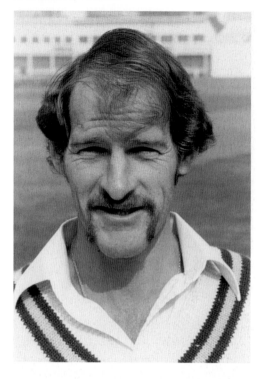

Born: 23 July 1949, Johannesburg, South Africa

Batting

M	I	NO	Runs	HS
283	450	65	17053	246
273	*266*	*41*	*8606*	*130*

Ave	50	100	ct/st	
44.29	85	37	268	
38.24	*59*	*7*	*105*	

Bowling

Runs	Wkts	Av	BB	5wI	10wM
11227	476	23.58	6-16	12	-
6577	*291*	*22.60*	*6-18*	*4*	-

Best Performances

246 v. Sussex, Hove, 1976
130 v. Scotland, Glasgow, 1982
6-16 v. Worcestershire, Worcester, 1977
6-18 v. Sussex, Hove, 1982

The departure of Gary Sobers in 1974, coupled with no fundemental improvement in the county's fortunes, appeared to herald once again a troubled future for the county. The overseas successor to Sobers, the Transvaal all-rounder Clive Rice, a hard-hitting batsman and a hostile fast-medium bowler signed by Jack Bond as his major legacy to the county, was an unknown quantity, with many supporters being unaware of his record or ability. Rice was quickly to establish his credentials as a fine all-rounder, claiming 5-46 in only his third Championship outing, eventually finishing top of the county's bowling averages. His determination to never concede defeat was evident in his maiden hundred for the county against Northamptonshire. On a seaming pitch, Notts were dismissed for 67, with Rice alone reaching double figures with 27. Requiring 235 to win, his unbeaten 109 in 285 minutes – a highly patient innings for such a positive player – gave Notts a five-wicket victory. In contrast his aggressive qualities were highlighted in his career-best 246 against Sussex at Hove in 300 minutes, his 6 sixes and 32 fours reminiscent of Alletson's great innings there in 1911. His unbeaten 213 against Glamorgan in 1978, one

of two double-centuries that season, was even quicker. Reaching 200 in 194 minutes, the quickest double-century by a Nottinghamshire player, his 1 six and 35 fours constituted over 68 per cent of his innings. A day earlier his unbeaten 120 against the same side had included 4 sixes and 13 fours, the highest innings by a Nottinghamshire batsman in the Sunday League.

His first three years had seen him top the county's bowling averages with a career-best 6-16 against Worcestershire in 1977. In that year he also topped the county's batting averages, coupling this with 814 runs in the Sunday League, at that time a record for the competition. A run of seven innings of over fifty in eight innings, including two consecutive hundreds, was another new first for this competition. This positive approach won him the captaincy in 1978 but his involvement with Packer's World Series resulted in his sacking before he could take up the position. Legal action forced the club to reinstate him as a player if not as captain. Rice responded by enjoying his greatest season with the bat, heading the national averages with 1,871 runs at an average of 66.82 and scoring 120* in the John Player League, another Nottinghamshire record.

Clive Rice's aggressive approach was a key factor in the county's success in the 1980s.

Rice contributed in full measure to both Championship successes in 1981 and 1987. Restored to the captaincy in 1979, he reached his pinnacle as an all-rounder in 1981, heading the batting averages with an average of 56.23, hitting 6 hundreds, taking most catches in the field and recording his best return of wickets, 65 at under 20 apiece. He also set a new world record with an unbeaten 105 out of 143 against Hampshire, the lowest total to contain a century. It was suggested in *Wisden* that here was the most complete player in world cricket. The following season Rice almost took Notts to a second consecutive Championship success. Requiring 297 off 60 overs to beat Somerset in the final fixture, he led the way with 98 off 109 balls, only for Notts to fall three runs short. He was less influential in 1987, his final season with the county, although he still managed to make 1,000 runs, the thirteenth season in succession, and a Nottinghamshire record. His bowling was less fiery, injuries having taken their toll over the years, but he was still as sharp in the field, for the sixth time holding the most catches. It was entirely in character that he struck an unbeaten hundred in his final appearance, ensuring maximum batting points that virtually guaranteed the Championship title. His contribution of 63 in the victorious NatWest final, although overshadowed by Hadlee's match winning innings, also kept Notts' slim hopes alive as wickets tumbled at the other end.

In his thirteen seasons, in nine of which he captained the side, he was the most consistent member of the team, scoring 1,000 runs every year and taking fifty or more wickets on four occasions. His average of 44.29 is the third highest for the county. His contribution in limited-overs cricket is equally impressive; at one stage in 1982 he held four of the six county records, two for batting and two for bowling. In the Sunday League he still retains the county record for most runs and most wickets in a season and in a career, and the highest innings and best bowling performances in the Benson & Hedges Cup. The amount of cricket he played was prodigious. He began by making 101 consecutive Championship appearances, in his first eight seasons missing only one match and over thirteen seasons missing only 14 out of 286. His 273 limited-overs games meant he was playing in well over forty games a season, as well as appearing for Transvaal in the winter.

Above all, his personal example gave back to the county a winning attitude which had been rarely felt since 1945. His inspirational approach in these years was to persuade the Committee to bring him back to Trent Bridge in 1999 as Director of Cricket in an attempt to re-galvanise the team. It was not to be a fairy-tale ending, for in spite of many changes to the playing staff, there was little improvement in the county's playing record. It was ironic that after Rice's removal in mid-2002, the side that he had put together should secure promotion to the First Division of the Championship. His selection of many of these players may still prove a significant contribution to the county's advance in the future.

Born: 23 June 1890, Radcliffe-on-Trent, Nottinghamshire

Died: 29 December 1957, Saxondale, Nottinghamshire

Batting

M	I	NO	Runs	HS
245	268	112	1532	70
Ave	50	100	ct/st	
9.82	2	-	37	

Bowling

Runs	Wkts	Av	BB	5wI	10wM
24184	1148	21.06	9-21	87	19

Best Performances

70 v. Derbyshire, Worksop, 1922

9-21 v. Hampshire, Nottingham, 1922

Len 'Tich' Richmond made his county debut in the penultimate county match of the 1913 season, 'after wonderful success in local cricket', but it was only after the First World War with Wass and Iremonger retired that he became one of the mainstays of the Notts attack. Until the mid-1920s he was to be the county's most successful bowler, taking more wickets than any other bowler in the side in the seven seasons from 1919 to 1926.

A small man, about 5ft 7in tall, he bowled a genuine controlled leg-break, mixed in with a well-disguised googly. As with most bowlers of his kind he was occasionally punished but on his day, and aided by helpful conditions, he was capable of running through a side. Against Gloucestershire on a rain-affected pitch in 1925, he took 14-83 in a day, his best match return for the county. From 1919, he proceeded to take over 100 wickets in the following seven seasons; in 1922 he experienced his greatest year, taking 169 wickets at a cost of only 13.48 apiece and finishing as the third most successful bowler in the country. It surpassed the 163 by Wass in 1907 and remained a county record until Dooland's 181 in 1954. It was also the year

which saw him return his best innings figures, 9-21 against Hampshire at Trent Bridge, which is still the best performance by a Notts bowler against that county. His 9-55 against Northamptonshire in 1925 made him only the fourth Nottinghamshire bowler to take nine wickets in an innings twice. On six occasions he was to claim eight wickets in an innings, twice taking three wickets in four balls as well as a hat-trick against Lancashire in 1926. His last successful season came in 1926, when he claimed 149 wickets, which is still the sixth highest number in a season by a Notts bowler.

His fall from grace was rapid as his bowling skills went into decline as his weight increased; 1928 was to be his final season, even though he still claimed sixty wickets, albeit rather expensive ones. The fact that Richmond was an abysmal batsman and a mediocre fielder also made him dispensable. It was reported in the *Cricketer* that he had been found a place in the field, deep third man, 'where he is not likely to have a catch'. It was certainly a factor in his being selected for only one Test, appearing against Australia at Trent Bridge in 1921. His first-class career, given the type of bowler he was and the success he obtained, was comparatively short, but he still remains the county's seventh highest wicket taker. He was, however, to remain a full-time cricketer for many more years, becoming employed by Sir Julien Cahn and a regular member of his side.

Robert Timothy Robinson
RHB & RM, 1978-99

Born: 21 November 1958, Skegby, Sutton-in-Ashfield, Nottinghamshire

Batting

M	I	NO	Runs	HS
374	651	77	24439	220*
362	352	39	10970	139

Ave	50	100	ct/st
42.57	130	55	238
35.04	70	9	109

Bowling

Runs	Wkts	Av	BB	5wI	10wM
274	4	68.50	1-22	-	-

Best Performances
220* v. Yorkshire, Nottingham, 1990
139 v. Worcestershire, Worcester, 1985
1-22 v. Northamptonshire, Northampton, 1982

Tim Robinson was one of the most reliable and consistent batsmen in Nottinghamshire's history, achieving both the second highest aggregate of runs and total of centuries for the county. Considering that Robinson also shouldered the responsibilities of captaincy for eight seasons and was also absent for many fixtures on international duty, these figures represent an impressive performance over his twenty-two seasons with the county.

His talents were first spotted whilst at Dunstable GS, giving him opportunities with Northamptonshire Second XI at the age of sixteen. On his return to Nottinghamshire he appeared for the county's Second XI, but delayed his county career until the completion of his studies at Sheffield University, when he became a regular member of the side, being involved in the Championship winning side in 1981 and appearing in the Benson & Hedges final the following year. His breakthrough season came in 1983, when he headed the batting averages, something he was to do on five subsequent occasions, scoring over 1,500 runs. It began a sequence of 1,000 plus runs in thirteen consecutive seasons, consistently averaging over forty with the bat and on six occasions over fifty. Only in 1987, when he was called up for the five Tests against Pakistan, did he fail to achieve 1,000 runs in county matches alone.

He was capped in 1983 after achieving his first double-century, 207 against Warwickshire – an early indication of his ability to play a big innings. He followed this in 1984 with over 2,000 runs, the first batsman since Mike Harris in 1971 to reach this target. By this time he and Chris Broad had formed a new opening partnership that was to eventually share twenty century stands in 124 first-wicket partnerships, finishing with an average of 52.50 runs per innings, by far the best for any Nottinghamshire openers. They began in splendid fashion in their first outing together, enjoying two century partnerships against Oxford University, only the fourth pair of Nottinghamshire batsmen to do so. Robinson went on to achieve this feat with two other opening partners, Dowman in 1995 and Pollard in 1989, in the latter instance sharing a unique county Championship record of two double-century partnerships against Kent at Trent Bridge.

Chosen to tour India in 1984/85, his 160 in his second Test appearance and a series average of 63.42 confirmed Robinson's place in the England side against the visiting Australians in 1985. His ability to go on to big scores was confirmed by his 175 in his first innings of the series and his 148 in the Fifth Test when he and Gower added 331 for the second wicket. In eleven Tests he had scored 934 runs at an average of 62.26, one of the best starts in Test history. Equally impressive was his calm temperament, his composure at the

Tim Robinson, one of the successful batsmen in the county's long history.

Australia, he, along with his county colleagues French and Broad, all in and out of the England side for several years, bowed out of Test cricket in 1989 when they opted to join the rebel tour to South Africa.

None of this affected Robinson's county form, even after he assumed the county captaincy in 1988. A stormy start was followed by years of relative success in the Championship. In his eight years at the helm, Notts finished in the top five on four occasions as well as winning the Benson & Hedges Cup in 1989 and the Sunday League in 1991. Robinson continued to score well over 1,000 runs a season, hitting a career-best unbeaten 220 against Yorkshire in 1990 and his third double-hundred, 209 against Northamptonshire in 1995, a season in which he scored seven hundreds. Two hundreds against Kent in 1990 and against Glamorgan in 1993 made him the third Notts batsman to have accomplished this on three occasions. Only Hampshire eluded his completion of a full set of hundreds against the other sixteen counties.

His ability to pace an innings also stood him in good stead in limited-overs cricket. In 1985, it was Robinson's efforts, which gained them a place in the NatWest final with three consecutive Man of the Match awards, the last one for a perfectly timed 139 against Worcestershire in the semi-final. In that year alone he scored 937 runs in limited-overs cricket at an average of 104.25. If his 80 in the 1985 final failed to secure victory, his 89 in the 1989 Benson & Hedges final that won him the Gold Award paved the way for Hemming's victorious boundary from the last ball against the same opponents. He is one of only three Nottinghamshire batsmen to have scored over 20,000 first-class runs and over 10,000 in limited-overs cricket for the county.

Quiet and introspective, always appearing very serious at the crease, he never fully established a close rapport with the Nottinghamshire supporters. He was, however, respected as a high-class batsman who was an integral part of the county's success in the 1980s. He is on the verge of returning to the first-class game, albeit as an umpire.

wicket and his repertoire of delightful shots. A reputation as an accumulator of runs, stemming from his eight and a half hours at the wicket for his 160 in India, had cast him as a crease occupier with few shots. His innings against Australia proved that he was also an attractive and stylish batsman, a beautiful timer of the ball who was always prepared to hit the bad ball. He was never a spectacular hitter, although he did produce one remarkable innings in New Zealand in 1987/88 when he struck 10 sixes and 13 fours in 166 against Northern Districts.

His Test future as an England opener now seemed assured but, although *Wisden* awarded him the accolade of one of its Five Cricketers of the Year, it warned that 'the ultimate test ... lay ahead in the West Indies in early 1986'. It was a test which Robinson was to fail spectacularly, alongside every other England batsmen, against the West Indian pace attack. He never again retained the full confidence of the England selectors, despite maintaining his form in domestic cricket and scoring a further big hundred against Pakistan. Left out of the home series against West Indies and the 1986/87 tour of

William Henry Scotton
LHB & LFM, 1875-90

Born: 15 January 1856, Nottingham
Died: 9 July 1893, St John's Wood, London

Batting

M	I	NO	Runs	HS
153	233	25	4144	110*

Ave	50	100	ct/st
19.92	16	2	74

Bowling

Runs	Wkts	Av	BB	5wI	10wM
200	5	40.00	1-16	-	-

Best Performances
Batting: 110* v. Surrey, Nottingham, 1886
Bowling: 1-16 v. Middlesex, Nottingham, 1882

William Scotton, a future England player, along with Arthur Shrewsbury and William Barnes, made his debut in 1875. It took Scotton four years to establish himself in the county side, when still only twenty-three he scored three fifties, including an unbeaten 84* against Middlesex at Trent Bridge, finishing second in the county's batting averages. Several references were made to his free hitting, Richard Daft commenting that in his day Scotton was 'one of the fastest run-getters and hardest hitters in the country'. In the early 1880s, Scotton's batting underwent a transformation, his aggressive approach being replaced by an ultra-negative one. Whether his absence from several matches in 1883 through poor health prompted a decision to ensure his future place by other methods is unclear, but his subsequent success clearly reinforced this change of approach. *Wisden* noted that in 1884 'of all the Notts batsmen not one made so remarkable progress as Scotton' and 'his title to be ranked as the best left-handed batsman in England is indisputable'. Second only to Shrewsbury in the county averages, he recorded his first century, an unbeaten 104* against Middlesex at Lord's, described as one of the best innings he had ever played. He again enjoyed an excellent season in 1886, carrying his bat for the first of four occasions, three times for Nottinghamshire, making 110* against Surrey at Trent Bridge. His 628 runs marked his most fruitful season for the county, whilst in all matches he fell just 21 runs short of 1,000 runs for the season.

It was in these years that Scotton produced his best displays for England, performances that earned him a reputation as one of the great stonewallers. At The Oval in 1884 he scored 90 in 340 minutes, assisting in securing a draw, which gave England the Ashes. It inspired a poem in *Punch*, which began 'Block, block, block, O Scotton!' and ended 'But one hour of Grace or Walter Read were worth a week of you.' Two years later in an opening partnership of 170 with W.G. Grace, a Test record, Scotton took 225 minutes over his 34, spending 67 minutes on 24; the first occasion a batsman in Tests had failed to score a run in sixty or more minutes. A year earlier he had also failed to score a run in 60 minutes against Gloucestershire at Trent Bridge, a unique achievement for a Nottinghamshire batsman. In all he played fifteen times for England.

Scotton proved a valuable opening batsman for the county, his best years being with Arthur Shrewsbury. He was an essential component of the great county side which between 1884 and 1886 – Scotton's best years – lost only one match. His ending was a tragic one. In 1893 he committed suicide by cutting his throat, the coroner suggesting that losing his place in the Notts side had been a contributory factor. Even his obituary in *Wisden* struck a depressing note. 'He carried caution to such extremes that it was often impossible to take any pleasure in seeing him bat.'

Born: 1 July 1849, Nottingham
Died: 11 March 1894, Nottingham

Batting

M	I	NO	Runs	HS
164	251	20	4287	128*
Ave	**50**	**100**	**ct/st**	
18.55	16	4	91/4	

Bowling

Runs	Wkts	Av	BB	5wI	10wM
154	5	30.80	2-27	-	-

Best Performances

128* v. Gloucestershire, Nottingham, 1872
2-27 v. Lancashire, Manchester, 1877

John Selby was the first wicketkeeper to appear in an England side, although only by default, as the first choice, Pooley, had been detained in New Zealand on alleged criminal charges. Selby opened the innings and top-scored in England's second innings of the inaugural match of 1876/77, eventually appearing in six Tests, all in Australia and achieving a creditable Test average of 23.27.

The son of a well-known cricketer of the 1840s, William Selby, who had appeared once for Nottinghamshire, he made his debut in 1870, but achieved little of note until an undefeated 128* against Gloucestershire at Trent Bridge; Wyld's hundred in the same innings prevented him from becoming the first Notts batsman to score a century at Trent Bridge. This innings, coupled with a number of not-outs, thrust him into second place in the leading averages behind W.G. Grace. A disastrous 1873 led to his being omitted for the whole of 1874 but given another chance in 1875 he performed well enough to rescue his career, essentially remaining an automatic choice for the remainder of his time with Nottinghamshire, excepting 1881, when he was one of the seven players involved in the Nottinghamshire professionals strike. His regular place in the side was helped considerably by his undoubted ability in the field, with *Wisden* stating that at times his fielding was 'unsurpassably brilliant'. This refers to his exceptional speed in the outfield, where it is claimed he saved hundreds of runs. Selby was in fact a pro-fessional sprinter, known as 'Bendigo's Novice', his patron being the famous prize-fighter. During the tour of Australia in 1876/77 he organised races between himself and the various local champions, probably for side bets.

His best year came in 1878 when he recorded the county's only hundred of the season, 107 against Yorkshire at Sheffield, and just missed by four runs a second hundred against Middlesex at Trent Bridge. In addition he made 66 against the visiting Australians, the first ever fifty scored against the Australians in England. With a century and 5 fifties to his name he topped the county averages for the only time in his career. Added to two excellent innings of 88 and 64 for the Players against the Gentlemen, he was to head the national batting averages, the first Nottinghamshire batsman to do so, scoring 938 runs at an average of 31.26. In 1879 he and William Oscroft put on 192 for the second wicket against Kent at Canterbury, at that time the highest partnership for any wicket for the county. A key member of the highly successful Nottinghamshire side of the early 1880s, his increasingly erratic batting performances (he registered 6 noughts in 19 innings in 1886) saw him left out of the side in 1887. His final years were touched by talk of financial misdemeanours. He was to face criminal charges in 1893, and although acquitted, it was asserted in *Wisden* that this was a contributory factor to his fatal stroke the following year.

Francis Joseph Shacklock
RHB & RF, 1883-93

Born: 22 September 1861, Crich, Derbyshire
Died: 1 May 1937, Christchurch, New Zealand

Batting

M	I	NO	Runs	HS
117	164	18	1847	71
Ave	50	100	ct/st	
12.65	1	-	72	

Bowling

Runs	Wkts	Av	BB	5wl	10wM
6745	360	18.73	8-32	27	6

Best Performances
71 v. Gloucestershire, College Close, Clifton, 1887
8-32 v. MCC, Lord's, 1887

Controversy was part and parcel of Frank (pictured extreme right, top row) Shacklock's up-and-down first-class career in England, the cricketer whose name is reputed to be linked with that of Mordecai Sherwin to form the first name of Conan Doyle's fictional character, Sherlock Holmes. Born in Derbyshire of Nottinghamshire parents, he was to appear for both counties, causing considerable friction between the two. He made a promising debut for Nottinghamshire against MCC in the final game of 1883 at Lord's when he took 5-48 in the match, but he opted to play for Derbyshire in 1884. With hindsight it was a shrewd move as the county, possessing a formidable attack, fielded an almost unchanged side in 1884 and 1885. Shacklock prospered in 1885, with his bowling going from strength to strength, whereupon he returned to his former county in 1886. Derbyshire complained to Lord's about the loss of their most promising bowler, with his departure subsequently proving an important factor in the removal of first-class status from the county in 1887.

Shacklock was a tall right-arm fast bowler, with a slinging action, having the ability to swing the ball in from leg as well as being capable of bowling an off-break. On hard wickets, he often brought the ball up sharply. He was somewhat inconsistent, on occasions proving erratic and expensive and seemingly not able to string good performances together. This was illustrated in the first three years after his return, with Shacklock being left out of the side in 1888; performances such as 8-32 against MCC at Lord's in 1887, the best innings figures of his career, proved to be a one-off affair. All this changed in 1889, with Shacklock twice taking 10 wickets in a match against Surrey and finishing with 80 wickets at 15.17 apiece. From then onwards he continued to take wickets, proving devastating on his day.

One great moment came against Surrey at The Oval in 1892, when in a vital Championship game he claimed match figures of 10-110 to assist Notts to a 4-wicket victory. His best match analysis for Notts was 12-166 against Sussex at Hove in 1892 and in the following season he took 8 wickets in an innings for the fourth and last time. This 8-46 against Somerset at Trent Bridge included 4 wickets in 4 balls, all clean bowled. It was the fifth instance in first-class cricket and only achieved once more by a Nottinghamshire bowler, A.K. Walker in 1956. It was his last great performance for the county; against Kent at Canterbury towards the end of the season, he failed to bowl in the second innings. It was reported to the committee that this was the consequence of drinking, and this not being the first occasion, he was subsequently released. After a spell with Nelson, he emigrated to New Zealand 'in rather murky circumstances', appearing for Otago and becoming a respected coach.

Alfred Shaw
RHB & RM/SM, 1864-97

Born: 29 August 1842, Burton Joyce, Nottinghamshire
Died: 16 January 1907, Gedling, Nottinghamshire

Batting

M	I	NO	Runs	HS
193	269	53	3269	88
Ave	50	100	ct/st	
15.13	6	-	188	

Bowling

Runs	Wkts	Av	BB	5wI	10wM
10342	899	11.50	8-25	82	19

Best Performances
88 v. Middlesex, Nottingham, 1882
8-25 v. Derbyshire, Derby, 1875

According to his obituary in *Wisden*, Alfred Shaw was one of the greatest figures in modern cricket. During his long first-class career that stretched over 34 seasons, the 'Emperor of bowlers' set a host of new records, both at county and Test level. He bowled the first ball in Test cricket, as well as becoming the first England bowler to take five wickets in an innings. He was the first bowler to claim two hat-tricks in a match, following this with three wickets in four balls in the same game, a unique achievement. He was to bowl more overs than runs conceded, an incredible performance even in the age of the four-ball over.

Alfred Shaw was a local cricketer who first attracted attention in 1863 when taking 7-14 for the Colts against Nottinghamshire. The following year he made his debut at Trent Bridge against Kent, claiming 6-31 but such was the strength of Nottinghamshire bowling, he was not asked to bowl in his first three appearances for the county. It was only in 1870 at the age of twenty-seven that he made his breakthrough as a recognised bowler, playing twenty games and taking 93 wickets and only with the retirement of first Grundy and then Wootton by 1871 did he begin to play a full part in the Nottinghamshire attack.

Shaw began as a round-arm medium-pace bowler but as his pace decreased, so his spin and break developed; Shaw spinning the ball sharply on helpful pitches in his later years. His great strength, however, whatever his pace, was his accuracy and his control over line and length. It was reputed that he never bowled a wide during his long career. Possessing a relaxed and easy action, he was able to bowl for long spells, bowling wicket to wicket and concentrating on bowling at the stumps. One of his most remarkable feats was for Notts against MCC at Lord's in 1875, when his 166 balls produced an analysis of 7-7 against a side containing W.G. Grace; Grace hit only three singles off Shaw in 70 minutes. In that game Shaw bowled twenty consecutive four-ball maidens, the most by any bowler, and beating his own record a year later with twenty-three consecutive maidens for the North against the South at Trent Bridge. Shaw had a more than useful record against Grace, bowling him on twenty occasions and dismissing him in 49 of the 144 innings in which they met. Grace was indeed aware of Shaw's legendary accuracy, observing that 'the great power of his bowling lay in its good length and unerring precision ... an impatient batsman might make two sparkling hits in succession off him, but he would not make a third.' His work rate was prodigious, in 1875 bowling more balls in a season than any other and one year later becoming the first bowler to

Alfred Shaw, the 'Emperor of bowlers.'

bowl over 2,000 four-ball overs; his grand total of 10,526 balls in 28 games, 1,000 more than any other bowler, was the most in a season until it was surpassed in 1928 by A.P. Freeman.

He was to take 100 wickets in a season in all matches on nine occasions, the first time in 1871; his best season being 1878 when he claimed 201 wickets at a cost of 10.96 apiece, the second time a bowler had taken over 200 first-class wickets in a season. His 186 wickets in 1880 at 8.54 apiece remains the lowest recorded average by a bowler taking 100 wickets in a season. For Nottinghamshire Shaw was the county's most successful bowler for seven seasons between 1873 and 1884, and he headed the national bowling averages in the latter year at the age of forty-two. He was also the first bowler to claim a hat-trick for the county, against Derbyshire at Derby in 1875. His best year was 1878 when he took 92 wickets, the same year he returned his best figures, 8-25 against Derbyshire at Derby. His best match return of 14-65 came in 1884 against Gloucestershire at Trent Bridge, the game in which he claimed two hat-tricks and three wickets in four balls. In this game he bowled unchanged throughout the match with Attewell, one of twelve instances in which Shaw achieved this feat. He enjoyed a highly successful opening partnership with Fred Morley, the pair bowling unchanged throughout both innings in six county matches in 1878 and 1879 as well as twice for MCC in 1880, a record for one pair of bowlers. After being one of the prime movers in the Nottinghamshire strike of 1881 by the leading professionals, according to *Wisden* 'the only regrettable incident in his career,' Shaw took over the captaincy. Under his leadership Nottinghamshire were generally accepted as the Champion county in five consecutive years between 1882 and 1886.

Shaw's services were much in demand and he was to appear in 404 first-class games in his career spanning four decades. Playing for MCC against the North at Lord's in 1874, he achieved career-best figures of 10-73. Shaw was also instrumental in organising the visits of touring sides to Australia, assisting in the promotion of four tours to Australia, the first of which in 1876/77 included the first two Test matches. In the second tour of 1881/82 he captained the side, becoming the first Nottinghamshire player to captain England.

At the age of forty-five he dropped out of the Nottinghamshire XI but continued to flourish with Sussex. In 1894, aged fifty-one, Shaw topped their bowling averages. Having been deprived of the captaincy by the Nottinghamshire committee against his wishes, he would have enjoyed taking 7-34 against his old county at Trent Bridge. The following season against Nottinghamshire he sent down 501 balls in the first innings, the most by any bowler in a Championship match until 1997.

One of a small number of bowlers to take over 2,000 wickets, he is the most economical of all, his 2,027 wickets costing a mere 12.12 apiece. After giving up playing, Shaw continued to be involved in cricket, being a first-class umpire until the end of the 1905 season.

Born: 11 April 1836, Sutton-in-Ashfield, Nottinghamshire
Died: 7 March 1888, Sutton-in-Ashfield, Nottinghamshire

Batting

M	I	NO	Runs	HS
69	101	38	244	11
Ave	50	100	ct/st	
3.87	-	-	37	

Bowling

Runs	Wkts	Av	BB	5wI	10wM
5288	422	12.53	9-86	40	14

Best Performances
11 v. Yorkshire, Sheffield, 1871
9-86 v. Gloucestershire, Nottingham, 1871

'Jemmy' Shaw (pictured standing, third from left) was one of the worst batsmen ever to appear for Nottinghamshire, only once reaching double figures, whilst his fielding could at best be described as indifferent. In spite of these deficiencies as a cricketer, from making his debut in 1865 at the comparatively late age of twenty-nine, he was to play in 68 consecutive matches, missing two games in 1875 before making his final appearance for Notts at Lord's against the MCC.

Shaw was a fast left-arm bowler with a high round-arm delivery; he whipped his arm over rapidly from behind when delivering the ball, often disconcerting batsmen early in their innings. Even W.G. Grace admitted that at times he was difficult to play and statistically Shaw was one of the most successful bowlers against him, capturing his wicket 28 times in the 63 times they met, and dismissing him four times for nought. At times he proved extremely difficult to score off, conceding only three scoring strokes off 100 balls against Kent at Trent Bridge in 1870, and finishing with an analysis of 4-5.

He made an immediate impact in 1865, taking 44 wickets in six appearances and heading the national averages with an average of 10.81. On his fourth appearance with Grundy he bowled unchanged to dismiss Yorkshire for 53, Shaw's match figures being 12-85, and in the following fixture against Cambridgeshire, he recorded match figures of 10-57 as he and Jackson bowled out their opponents for 64. The final game of the season saw Shaw's bowling unchanged, this time with Chris Tinley as Sussex was put out for 77. He again topped the county's averages in 1866, taking the most wickets (35), and was to continue in this vein until almost the end of his career. He was the first county bowler to claim over fifty wickets in a season for Nottinghamshire, achieving this in three consecutive seasons from 1869 to 1871; his most productive season was 1870, when he claimed 62 victims. He was the county's leading bowler in five of his eleven seasons, capturing five wickets in an innings on forty occasions out of the 125 innings in which he bowled, the largest number by any Nottinghamshire bowler at that time. His best innings figures were 9-86 against Gloucestershire at Trent Bridge in 1871 and in the same year he returned his best match figures for the county, 13-58 against Surrey, also at Trent Bridge.

He was a regular member of the All England XI, appearing for them until 1886, and he returned some impressive figures in representative games, such as 8-19 for the North against the South in 1869, bowling sixteen consecutive maidens and dismissing W.G. for nought. His record of 5 wickets in an innings on 59 occasions in 115 appearances is one to be proud of, whilst the times he failed to take a wicket in a match could be numbered on the fingers of one hand.

Mordecai Sherwin
RHB & RF/WK, 1876-96

Born: 26 February 1851, Greasley, Nottinghamshire
Died: 3 July 1910, Nottingham

Batting

M	I	NO	Runs	HS
206	276	89	1444	35
Ave	50	100	ct/st	
7.72	-	-	387/113	

Bowling

Runs	Wkts	Av	BB	5wI	10wM
42	5	8.40	2-7	-	-

Best Performances
35 v. Surrey, The Oval, 1885
2-7 v. Kent, Nottingham, 1888

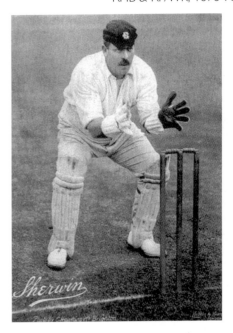

The early retirement and death of Nottinghamshire's regular 'keeper Sam Biddulph in 1876 left the county with an unexpected vacancy. Sherwin, a local cricketer who had pressed his claims with the county club for a position, was brought in as a stop-gap measure towards the end of the season and for a number of matches the following season. Although recognised as the better 'keeper, Sherwin was kept out of the Notts XI for the next two seasons by Wyld, a far superior batsman, only securing a regular place when Wyld's form deteriorated, remaining the automatic choice as 'keeper until 1893.

Sherwin was one of the heaviest wicketkeepers on record, his weight gradually increasing over the years from 14st to 17st. Even so, according to W.G. Grace, he was 'as nimble and sharp as a cat and took any bowling with absolute ease and certainty'. He was especially proficient at taking balls down the leg-side and was also noted for his courage, often standing up to the fastest bowling. 'Nowt fears me,' he is reported to have said when being interviewed for a position at Trent Bridge. He was a highly extrovert character, who often played to the crowd. On his day he ranked with the best 'keepers of his day, playing in three Tests: twice on the 1886/87 tour of Australia and once at Lord's in 1888. His abilities were recognised in his selection for the Players in eleven consecutive games from 1883.

His arrival coincided with Nottinghamshire's greatest years. He was an ever-present in the champion team of 1884 and took over the captaincy in 1887 when Shrewsbury declined the offer, holding it for two seasons. He led the side on thirty-five occasions, until replaced by the amateur J.A. Dixon, thus becoming the last appointed professional captain until 1961. His 50 dismissals in 1887 were the most in a season by a Notts 'keeper. Grace considered this a remarkable record, stating that 'few players can take that responsibility on their shoulders and play up to their best form'. Two years later he dismissed eight batsmen, five caught and three stumped, in the match against Gloucestershire at Trent Bridge, his best performance for the county and a county record until 1906. Sherwin remained a regular choice until 1893 when he was left out of the side, returning to play in only one further game, his benefit match in 1896.

In addition to his prowess at cricket, Sherwin played for Notts County as a goalkeeper. During his cricketing career he was also the landlord of a number of Nottingham public houses and also stood unsuccessfully as a local councillor. On retirement he became a first-class umpire and was rewarded with being chosen to stand in the first ever Test match staged at Trent Bridge in 1899. He was the first Nottinghamshire 'keeper to claim 500 dismissals for the county, one of only five to have reached this figure.

Born: 11 April 1856, New Lenton, Nottinghamshire
Died: 19 May 1903, Gedling, Nottinghamshire

Batting

M	I	NO	Runs	HS
375	574	59	19409	267
50	100	ct/st		
88	44	251		

Bowling

Runs	Wkts	Av	BB	5wI	10wM
2	0	-	-	-	-

Best Performances
267 v. Middlesex, Nottingham, 1887 and v. Sussex, Nottingham, 1890

Arthur Shrewsbury was an accumulator of records and runs at both county and international level. He was the first Test captain to score a century and the first to score 1,000 Test runs. For his county he scored its first double-century and was the first to complete 1,000 runs in a season. After the County Championship was reorganised in 1890, he was the first both to score 1,000 runs and a double-century. His average of 78.71 in 1887 was the highest ever and his eight centuries in that year equalled W.G. Grace's record number. He led England on seven occasions, being victorious in five of them, and was the last professional to captain England until Hutton in 1952.

Although it was sacrilegious to compare any batsman in the Victorian era with Grace, the latter graciously acknowledged Shrewsbury's status at that time with the oft-quoted remark 'Give me Arthur' when asked with which batsman he would prefer to open, Shrewsbury was certainly on figures alone the best batsman in England from 1885 to 1895. Between 1885 and 1892 he headed the batting averages six times, as

well as the Test averages in both 1886 and 1893.

He made his first-class debut in 1875 aged 18 years 3 days, the fourth youngest player to have appeared for Nottinghamshire at that time. An ever-present in his first season, he scored his maiden century in 1876 but, although making a number of impressive innings, he could not be described as a great run scorer until 1882. Ill health was a factor, underlined by his late arrival in Australia in 1881/82 after suffering from bronchitis. There he played in all four Tests, but the greatest legacy of the tour was the great improvement in his health. In 1882 he scored the first of his 10 double-centuries, culminating in a career-best 267 against Middlesex in 1887, the highest innings at Trent Bridge; a score he was to repeat against Sussex in 1890. In 1883 he passed 1,000 runs in a season for the first time, something he was to achieve on thirteen occasions. His great year was 1887, when he headed the national averages with his highest aggregate of runs (1653), scored 8 centuries, including three in consecutive innings at Lord's, and became the first batsman to score 1,000 runs exclusively in Nottinghamshire matches.

At the start of his career *Wisden* had observed that 'if followed by steadiness, practice and good conduct, his form bids fair to place him in the front rank of batting professionals'. All three, added to his natural ability, were highly important ingredients in his success.

Arthur Shrewsbury, the greatest professional batsman of his day.

A deep thinker about technique, he developed the art of playing off the back foot, rather than following the more popular front foot approach. Watching the ball carefully onto the bat, his immaculate defence was then supplemented by the innovation of pad-play, using the pad outside the off-stump as a second line of defence. Severely criticised at the time, it was Shrewsbury's counter to the growth of off-theory, the practice of bowlers to pitch the ball outside the off-stump to a packed offside field. This was a compliment to Shrewsbury's great skill on the leg-side, especially through mid-wicket, his *Times* obituary noting that 'the certainty with which he scored on the on side from any thing like a short-pitched ball being astonishing'. Neither tall nor physically strong, Shrewsbury relied on technique and timing to score his runs, stroking, steering and pushing, rather than hitting the ball. Unremitting practice in the winter allied to inexhaustible patience plus his defensive technique made him unrivalled on difficult pitches and when set on a good wicket extremely difficult to dismiss. His 164 in seven hours at Lord's in 1886 against Spofforth on a pitch all in favour of the bowlers was described as one of the finest ever. His confidence when well set is best illustrated by his comment to the Nottinghamshire dressing room attendant at the luncheon interval that he was to bring him out a cup of tea at four o'clock. It was a confidence shared by the Nottinghamshire side, most of whom allegedly went down to the beach when Shrewsbury and Gunn were batting together at Hove. He was the first batsman to bat for over ten hours, his 267 against Middlesex taking 615 minutes.

His determination to be the complete batsman was complimented by his approach to business and financial matters. He was involved in the organisation of four tours to Australia in the 1880s. He also played no first-class cricket in 1894 and cut down his appearances in 1895, in part as a consequence of his involvement in his business affairs with his sports firm, Shaw & Shrewsbury. He was at the forefront of disputes with the authorities over wages and appear-

ances, being one of the leaders of the 1881 strike of the Nottinghamshire professionals.

In 1902, aged forty-six, he headed the national batting averages for the last time, becoming the first Nottinghamshire batsman to score a century in both innings of a match. He became convinced that he was suffering from an incurable disease and at the beginning of the 1903 season shot himself. A complex character – teetotaller, non-smoker, bachelor, sensitive about his premature baldness to the point of not being seen without a hat, desperate to sleep at home if at all possible, continually worrying about his health and sight – Shrewsbury has been described as 'living a lonely life in the midst of crowds'. He was the greatest professional batsman of his day, whose run-getting achievements were complimented by a graceful and elegant style of batting. Siegfried Sassoon, cricket fanatic and war poet, was to write 'How I wished I could bat like him, if only for one day.'

Reginald Thomas Simpson
RHB & OB, 1946-63

Born: 27 February 1920, Sherwood Rise, Nottingham

Batting

M	I	NO	Runs	HS
366	630	42	23088	243*
Ave	50	100	ct/st	
39.26	120	48	142	

Bowling

Runs	Wkts	Av	BB	5wI	10wM
2073	50	41.46	3-22	-	-

Best Performances
243* v. Worcestershire, Nottingham, 1950
3-22 v. Warwickshire, Birmingham, 1949

Even before Reg Simpson made his Championship debut for the county midway through the 1946 season, there was considerable praise in many quarters for both his attractive stroke making and his run scoring, following a number of impressive performances whilst serving in the RAF in India and on leave in England in 1944. Simpson was to develop into a fine on-side hitter, not being afraid to lift the ball if necessary over mid-on, captains often placing this fielder twenty yards deeper when Simpson was at the crease. Most contemporaries agree he was one of the finest players of fast bowling, unruffled by the short-pitched bouncer, which he almost nonchalantly allowed to pass with a slight sway of the body. His ability against fast bowling was evident in his two seventies against the Australians in 1948, when Lindwall, letting himself go for the first time on the tour, took 6-14 in Nottinghamshire's first innings.

His attacking flair was soon apparent in his first Championship season, when after a very modest beginning, he made 201 in 245 minutes against Warwickshire at Trent Bridge, his maiden three-figure innings in first-class cricket It proved to be the first of 10 double-centuries, nine of them for Nottinghamshire, the highest number for the county. Simpson was selected for the MCC tour to South Africa in 1948/49,

enjoying a good tour but failing in his first and only Test appearance. There then followed two years in which he could do little wrong, finishing fourth and then second in the national batting averages. 1949 was a wonderful year, in which he enjoyed a sensational run of form, an unbeaten double-hundred against Surrey being followed with a later sequence of seven innings of fifty and over. This included a century in each innings of the match against Leicestershire, his second hundred coming in 100 minutes, he and Cyril Poole claiming victory with an unfinished second-wicket partnership of 251 in 97 minutes. He failed by only four runs to notch a third consecutive hundred in his next innings against Lancashire. However, Simpson made amends with his ninth score of fifty plus in ten innings with his highest innings so far, 238 against Lancashire at Old Trafford, part of a first-wicket partnership of 318 in 315 minutes with Keeton, their fourth consecutive century opening partnership. He began the 1950 season with a hundred in each of his first three games, this including an unbeaten 230* out of 352 against Glamorgan. He hit a century against the West Indian tourists and recorded his highest score so far, 243* against Worcestershire, the highest innings in the Championship that year, and went on to beat his 1949 aggregate of 2,525 by a further 51 runs. A Nottinghamshire player has never equalled his average of 85.13.

This was to be followed by his greatest Test performance during the tour of Australia in

Reg Simpson, one of the finest exponents of fast bowling.

1950/51. Prior to this tour he had appeared in five out of England's last six Tests, after a fine exhibition of attacking batsmanship in his second Test appearance and his first in England against New Zealand at Old Trafford in 1949, when he move from fifty to his initial Test hundred in a mere 27 minutes, striking 3 sixes off Burtt and being dismissed going for a fourth. Playing in every Test in Australia and scoring well over 1,000 runs on the tour, including a career-best 259 against New South Wales, his unbeaten 156* in the Fifth and final Test of the series assisted England to their first-ever victory against Australia since the end of the Second World War. A last wicket partnership of 74 with Tattersall in 55 minutes, Simpson scoring 64 of them, gave his side a precious first innings lead of 103, which proved vital to the outcome of the match. Although never again commanding a regular place in the England side, he was to score two more Test hundreds, both at Trent Bridge, as yet the only Nottinghamshire batsman to reach three figures on his home ground. At that time his 27 England caps equalled Voce's record of the most appearances by a Nottinghamshire player for his country.

Although appointed captain in 1951 the runs continued to flow, with over 2,000 in 1952 and 1953. It was a feat he was to achieve for the fifth and final time in 1959, when he recorded 2,033 runs in county matches alone, only the fourth Nottinghamshire batsman to do so. Still a positive batsman, in 1954 he struck 147 before lunch against Somerset on the first day, the most runs by any Nottinghamshire player in that particular session of play.

Having led the county on 249 occasions, a number surpassed only by A.O. Jones and Arthur Carr, Simpson gave up the captaincy in 1961. Unfortunately his era as captain coincided with one of the most depressing periods in the county's long history, apart from the Dooland years after 1957. A notorious featherbed Trent Bridge pitch coupled with an absence of penetrative bowlers made it almost impossible to the county to win a game at home. Simpson's frustration was evident when in 1951 he bowled a series of under-arm deliveries whilst playing against Glamorgan, but more significantly he became the driving force in persuading the club to take steps to dig up the square and start again.

His last three playing seasons were limited almost entirely to home games, with Simpson finishing top of the national batting averages in 1962 for the only time in his playing career with an average of 54.18. He remains the sixth highest run scorer in the county's history, having headed the county averages on seven occasions and being only the third Nottinghamshire batsman to score a century against every other county. He has remained a key figure in the county's subsequent history; a member of the committee from 1961 to 1986, the longest serving member on record, and being president for two years. Now an honorary vice-president, few in the county's history can have experienced such a long and distinguished connection with the Nottinghamshire club.

Born: 15 September 1927, Horsforth, Yorkshire

Batting

M	I	NO	Runs	HS
148	210	52	2347	64
Ave	50	100	ct/st	
14.85	4	-	56	

Bowling

Runs	Wkts	Av	BB	5wI	10wM
11179	367	30.46	10-66	18	4

Best Performances
64 v. Glamorgan, Nottingham, 1958
10-66 v. Gloucestershire, Stroud, 1956

When the Notts committee reluctantly gave up its long-held tradition of using only players with strong associations with the county, the first non-Nottinghamshire player to be specially registered was a twenyty-three-year-old off-spinner from Yorkshire, Ken Smales. Smales had joined the Yorkshire staff in 1948 but in three seasons had appeared in only thirteen games, his best performance for Yorkshire in 1950 being 5-44 against the West Indian tourists, this including three wickets in four balls. His first four seasons with the county were dismal ones. He was unable to command a regular place and the arrival of Dooland in 1953 saw him play no Championship cricket at all.

It was not until August 1954 that he first took five wickets in an innings but he then cemented a regular place in the side, being ever present in both 1955 and 1956. In the former season he claimed over a hundred wickets for the only time in his career, as the Nottinghamshire pitches became more bowler friendly. He claimed ten wickets in a match for the first time against Derbyshire, repeating the feat against Somerset and also turned in a career-best 7-44 against Derbyshire at Trent Bridge, six times surpassing his previous career-best performance set the previous season.

The year 1956 also began promisingly with match figures of 11-93 against Surrey at home but the highpoint of his career came eighteen days later against Gloucestershire at Stroud in the first ever fixture played on that ground. After Nottinghamshire had been dismissed for a mediocre total, Smales, coming on as second change, took the first four Gloucestershire wickets by the close of the first day and a fifth early on the second day. A sixth wicket partnership of 103 took the home side well past the Nottinghamshire total but Smales then took the remaining five, which fell for a mere 16 runs. His figures of 10-66 off 41.3 overs made him the first and as yet the only bowler to have taken ten wickets in an innings for the county. Perhaps even more remarkable in a match which the county lost easily by nine wickets was that Dooland had bowled 29 overs from the other end without taking a wicket.

An ever present in his final season, his 7-42 against Hampshire at Trent Bridge included a spell of five wickets for seven runs. After taking 5-59 in his final first-class game, he left the club to take up an appointment with Nottingham Forest FC. Smales was also a useful lower order batsman, his highest innings of 64 coming in his last season. He often proved a difficult batsman to prise out, as witnessed by almost a quarter of his innings being not-outs.

Aged only thirty-one, he could have given many more useful years to the county.

Michael John Smedley
RHB, 1964-79

Born: 28 October 1941, Maltby, Yorkshire

Batting

M	I	NO	Runs	HS
357	599	74	16414	149
206	197	28	3676	75
Ave	**50**	**100**	**ct/st**	
31.26	79	28	258	
21.75	14	-	55	

Bowling

Runs	Wkts	Av	BB	5wI	10wM
4	0	-	-	-	-

Best Performances
149 v. Glamorgan, Swansea, 1970
75 v. Gloucestershire, Nottingham, 1968

Mike Smedley was one of a number of ex-Yorkshire players in the early sixties to join the Nottinghamshire club, making his first-class debut in 1964 and one year later heading the county averages, having registered his maiden hundred against Derbyshire. Of all the young players, Smedley at twenty-three, was seen as the best future prospect in the team, not merely because of his early success but because he had impressed many critics with his technical ability and attractive style of batting. He was also a talented cover point, later moving into the slips, where he took over twenty catches in three separate seasons, ending as the county's ninth most successful fielder in terms of catches held. Confirmation of his early promise came in the following year, when he again topped the county's averages, making over 1,000 runs for the first time. In the next ten seasons he was to reach this target a further eight times with over 900 in the other two. His best season came in 1971 when he totalled 1,718 runs, averaging over forty for the only time in his career, and hit six Championship hundreds, including one in each innings against Lancashire at Old Trafford. Highly competent and reliable, he had made his thousand runs a season at around an average of thirty, scored his hundreds at about two a season but never seemed able to raise his game above this comfortable level. This was also reflected in his contribution in the various limited overs competitions, in which he averaged around twenty-one and never scored above 75.

From 1973 he was called upon to lead the side, firstly in the absence of Sobers, then as a stand in for Bond, scoring a century against the visiting West Indians on the first occasion he led the side. He captained the side for three years, being replaced by Rice in 1978, only to be reinstated before the season began, after Rice had signed for Packer. A tougher side began to evolve under the new manager, Ken Taylor, who felt that a more aggressive style of leadership was required, replacing Smedley by Rice in mid-1979. Having given up the captaincy once, it was one step too far for Smedley, who retired from the first-class game. His leadership had been as quiet, thoughtful and unobtrusive as his batting but like his batting was not inspirational, dominating or adventurous. In the event the decision to give Rice the captaincy proved the correct one but it was a sad end to Smedley's career with the county. Extremely reliable, he had played in all but 8 out of the 300 Championship games between being capped in 1966 and 1978, his last full year as captain. In a team which underwent many changes and achieved little success in these years, he remained one of the constant factors who still stands as the nineteenth highest run-scorer in the county's history.

Born: 28 July 1936, Bay Land, Bridgetown, Barbados

Batting

M	I	NO	Runs	HS
107	174	30	7041	160
86	85	19	2551	116*
Ave	**50**	**100**	**ct/st**	
48.89	25	18	111	
38.65	17	1	37	

Bowling

Runs	Wkts	Av	BB	5wI	10wM
7202	281	25.62	7-69	9	1
2227	103	21.62	5-43	1	-

Best Performances
160 v. Surrey, The Oval, 1970
116 v. Worcestershire, Newark, 1971*
7-69 v. Kent, Dover, 1968
5-43 v. Derbyshire, Chesterfield, 19697

In 1967 Nottinghamshire failed to win a Championship match, only just escaping last position in the table for the third consecutive year. Supporters were therefore elated by the news that the world's greatest all-rounder, Gary Sobers, was joining the county in 1968, a county against whom he struck 153 and 219* in past years. An offer of £5,000 a year, which made him the highest paid cricketer in the world, was enough to bring him to unfancied Nottinghamshire. The possessor of innumerable records, including the highest innings in Test cricket, there were suggestions that at the age of thirty-one, his best days were over. Yet Sobers was still to play in a further 28 Tests for West Indies, score seven more Test hundreds and take almost another 100 Test wickets.

Sobers was to spend seven seasons with Nottinghamshire, appearing in only 107 out of 160 possible Championship games. Appearances were restricted by both the West Indies tour of 1969 and 1973 and the Rest of the World matches in 1970. A knee injury also limited his games to six in 1972. However, an added bonus for the county was the extension of limited-overs cricket, the Gillette Cup being joined by the John Player League in 1969 and the Benson & Hedges Cup in 1972.

Hopes that Sobers might accomplish for Notts what he did for South Australia in 1963/64, who won the Sheffield Shield for the first time in eleven years, were not realised. Claiming fourth place in his first year, the county's highest position since 1932, a gradual decline left the county once again in last position in 1973, with Nottinghamshire winning only one game in both that year and the previous one. In that regard, the signing of Sobers could be termed a failure, with no lasting or deep impact on the club's fortunes. What his presence achieved was a revival of interest and enthusiasm amongst supporters who had seen little of note since the heady days of Dooland.

With a thousand new members signed up, Sobers immediately announced his presence by winning the Man of the Match award in a Gillette Cup game against Lancashire, taking a wicket before a run had been scored off him and then seeing Notts home with an unbeaten 75. He repeated the feat in the next round against Worcestershire, rescuing the county by coming in at 29/3 to score an unbeaten 95 and then took 4-15 off 11 overs, putting Notts into the third round for the first time. His immediate impact in the Championship was also impressive, his 5-25 against Middlesex making him the

Nottinghamshire supporters had the privilege of watching one of the world's greatest players for seven seasons.

first bowler to take five wickets on his Championship debut since Voce in 1928. He completed the match double of a century and ten wickets against Kent, surprisingly the only occasion in his first-class career he was to take ten or more wickets in a match. His 7-69 in the first innings was to be his best performance for Notts, whilst his unbeaten 105* was the fastest hundred of the season, Sobers taking only 77 minutes to reach three figures. It was a highly successful introduction to Championship cricket, during which he was to record his highest aggregate for the county, 1,570 runs at 44.85; bowl 773 overs, the most by any Notts bowler; take 83 wickets at 22.67 apiece; and claim 25 catches, the highest number for the county in 1968. He also appeared in more games in 1968 than he had done in any previous season. The climax of the season was his new world record in Nottinghamshire's final game of the season. Against Glamorgan at Swansea, Sobers came to the wicket with Notts on 308/5 and with a declaration in mind. He had faced nine overs and was unbeaten with 40 when he again faced the left-arm spin of Malcolm Nash, dispatching all six deliveries for six.

Although playing less cricket for the county in 1969 and 1970 due to international commitments, he still turned in some outstanding performances – a rapid century in even time against Surrey in 1969, 77 runs coming in boundaries, and a century in each innings against the same county the following season when no other Notts batsman made over forty. In 1970 he managed 5 hundreds in 14 Championship games, finishing with a staggering average of 76.93, which, along with his performances for the Rest of the World, took him to the head of the national batting averages. By these standards 1971 was relatively disappointing. For Sobers it was his most gruelling season for the county, captaining the side in 23 out of 24 Championship games as well as in 15 limited-overs fixtures. He still averaged 46.40 with the bat and claimed 53 wickets, albeit more expensive than normal, as well as becoming only the third player to score over 500 runs and take over twenty wickets in a John Player season, including the county's highest innings in that competition, an unbeaten 116 against Worcestershire. However, the strain of continuous cricket over so many years was beginning to tell. A damaged cartilage in the left knee, possible the consequence of bowling quickly off a required reduced run in the John Player League, reduced his appearances to six in 1972 and prompted a decision to give up the captaincy.

Sobers continued to top the county batting averages in his final two seasons with the club. In 1974 he again struck the quickest hundred of the year, reaching his century against Derbyshire in 83 minutes and with a final flourish in his last-ever first-class appearance, scored his eighty-sixth and final hundred against Lancashire at Old Trafford. It was achieved in typical Sobers fashion, his 132 including 3 sixes and 13 fours. His career average of 48.89 for the county, achieved solely in Championship games, was the highest achieved by any Nottingham-shire batsman. Nottinghamshire spectators were simply grateful to watch one of the game's greatest players in action on so many occasions.

Arthur Staples
RHB & RM, 1924-38

Born: 4 February 1899, Newstead Colliery,
Nottinghamshire
Died: 9 September 1965, Redhill, Nottingham

Batting

M	I	NO	Runs	HS
353	505	57	12457	153*
Ave	**50**	**100**	**ct/st**	
27.80	66	12	211	

Bowling

Runs	Wkts	Av	BB	5wI	10wM
18726	632	29.62	7-20	14	-

Best Performances
153* v. Cambridge University, Cambridge, 1936
7-20 v. Derbyshire, Nottingham, 1933

Arthur Staples followed his elder brother into the first team at the end of the 1924 season but unlike Sam, who became a permanent member of the team in his debut season in 1920, it took Arthur four seasons to establish himself in the side. Until then he tasted success as a Second XI player and often found himself in the position of twelfth man for the county side. Filling in when regular players were absent through injury, he proved himself an effective stop-gap player, turning in some useful performances with both bat and ball.

By 1928 his contributions as a useful lower-order batsman and as a medium-pace stock bowler in a strong bowling line-up earned him a regular place in the side. His future advance came mainly through his batting, although in Nottinghamshire's Championship-winning year of 1929, he was to take 82 wickets in all matches, his best-ever performance with the ball, as well as passing 1,000 runs for the first time and taking 30 catches. He could well be described as the side's best all-rounder at this time. He reached 1,000 runs in six further seasons, five times in Championship fixtures; his most productive season was 1932, when he scored 1,531 runs in all games. In that year he

had the bizarre distinction of making nine runs from a single stroke off Clark of Northamptonshire, the batsmen running five, followed by a return which resulted in four overthrows. In all he scored 12 hundreds for the county, ten in Championship matches, his first not coming until 1931, when, aged thirty-two, against Somerset at Trent Bridge, he was operating as a temporary opener. A year later his early season batting form won him a Test Trial, forcing him to miss his only Championship match between 1931 and 1935, during which time he made 119 consecutive appearances.

He retired from first-class cricket at the end of the 1938 season after being troubled by sciatica. He had also followed a career as a professional footballer, keeping goal for Mansfield Town and Bournemouth. Like his brother Sam, his all-round performances are best measured by his final career figures for the county. He was the eighth player to record over 5,000 runs and over 500 wickets for the county; he took 211 catches, still the fifteenth highest number by a Notts player; and he appeared in 353 matches, the thirteenth highest number by a county player at the time of his retirement.

Samuel James Staples
RHB & OB, 1920-34

Born: 18 September 1892, Newstead Colliery,
Nottinghamshire

Died: 4 June 1950, Nottingham

Batting

M	I	NO	Runs	HS
368	457	91	6248	110
Ave	50	100	ct/st	
17.07	19	1	329	

Bowling

Runs	Wkts	Av	BB	5wI	10wM
28874	1268	22.77	9-141	68	-

Best Performances

110 v. Surrey, The Oval, 1923
9-141 v. Kent, Canterbury, 1927

Sam Staples and later his younger brother Arthur were virtually automatic members of the highly successful county XI in the 1920s and '30s. Graduating from his colliery side, Sam made his debut in 1920, aged twenty-seven, his career having been delayed by the war years, and he immediately became a permanent member of the side. Only illness or injury were to keep him out of the eleven until his retirement in 1934. Altogether he was to make 385 appearances, at that time the sixth highest number for the county and still the thirteenth highest today.

Initially a support bowler for Barratt and Richmond, he was the last slow bowler to open the bowling for the county on a regular basis. Possessing a jumpy, shuffling run-up, redeemed by a beautiful action, he bowled slowish medium off-breaks and cutters, often resorting to round the wicket on helpful pitches. Acquiring a fine command of length over the years, he was able to bowl for long spells, effectively closing up one end, thus allowing the county's strike bowlers some breathing space. For many seasons he became the workhorse of the county's bowling, none more so than in 1927 when he was to bowl 1,233 Championship overs, twice as many as any other Notts bowler. It was to be his most productive year, his 127 wickets for the county including a career-best 9-141 against Kent at Canterbury on a pitch which gave him no help. It earned him a tour place to South Africa in 1928/29, where he appeared in three Tests with

some success, taking 15 wickets. He maintained his form the following season, taking over a hundred wickets for the fourth consecutive season, and was again chosen to tour, this time to Australia. Sadly he was stricken by muscular rheumatism and returned home without having made a single appearance on tour.

His consistent bowling form is reflected in his record of fifty or more wickets in thirteen of his fourteen full seasons, eleven of them yielding eighty-five or more wickets. Altogether he claimed 1,268 victims for the county, the fourth most successful Nottinghamshire bowler of all time. He also contributed useful runs during his career, never reaching 1,000 runs in a season but recording one first-class hundred against Surrey at The Oval in 1923. He featured in two century partnerships for the last wicket, one of which produced 140 in 60 minutes against Derbyshire at Worksop in 1922, underlying the aggressive nature of his batting.

As well as being one of only twelve players to have scored over 5,000 runs and taken over 500 wickets for the county, as a specialist slip fielder he held on to 329 catches, a total beaten by only three other fielders. He equalled A.O. Jones' record of 39 catches in a season in 1926 and took over thirty catches in a season on three other occasions. Sciatica forced his retirement in 1934, but he remained in the game in various capacities as a coach, scorer and first-class umpire.

Barry Stead
LHB & LFM, 1962-76

Born: 21 June 1939, Leeds, Yorkshire
Died: 15 April 1980, Drighlington, Yorkshire

Batting

M	I	NO	Runs	HS
215	230	73	1938	58
156	105	31	742	35*
Ave	**50**	**100**	**ct/st**	
12.34	2	-	53	
10.02	-	-	25	

Bowling

Runs	Wkts	Av	BB	5wI	10wM
16933	604	28.03	8-44	21	2
4578	199	23.00	5-26	3	-

Best Performances
58 v. Gloucestershire, Bristol, 1972
35 v. Middlesex, Newark, 1976*
8-44 v. Somerset, Nottingham, 1972
*5-26 v. Minor Counties, Newark, 1975 & 5-26 v.
  Essex, Nottingham, 1975*

One of the most enthusiastic bowlers to have played for the county, Barry Stead only achieved a reward for his efforts in the latter stages of his career. A small, stocky man, his attitude to the game was encapsulated in his whirlwind, rather frenetic approach to the wicket. His left-arm medium-fast bowling brought him a sensational first-class debut, when, aged twenty, he took 7-76 for Yorkshire against the Indians in 1959. The strength of the Yorkshire side at this time offering limited opportunities, Stead opted to play for Nottinghamshire.

He found it tough to break into the Nottinghamshire side, facing competition initially from Davison, Corran and Forbes, and later from Sobers and Halfyard. In 1967 a number of excellent performances, including at that time a career-best 7-32 against Worcestershire and 6-75 against his former county, appeared to have won him a permanent place but it was only in 1969, aged thirty and after taking most wickets in that year, that he became a virtually automatic choice. Capped in 1969, the climax of his career came in 1972, when appearing in every game, he fell two wickets short of what would have been a well-deserved 100 wickets in a season when no bowler reached that target for the first time since 1866. His figures of 12-111 in the opening fixture against Somerset marked the first time he had taken over ten wickets in a match. These included a career-best 8-44, the first occasion for fourteen years that a Notts bowler had taken eight wickets in an innings, and a hat-trick, his last victim being fellow-

Yorkshireman, Brian Close. It was also the year in which he celebrated his maiden fifty in only 43 minutes against Lancashire, followed by 58 against Gloucestershire, the highest innings of his career.

For the next three years he remained one of the county's leading wicket-takers, until first a hamstring injury during his benefit year of 1976 and then an Achilles tendon problem the following season effectively brought his first-class career to an end. During these later years he turned in some match-winning performances in limited-overs games. He became the first Notts bowler to take five wickets in a Gillette cup match, 5-44 against Worcestershire in 1974, and was also the first Notts bowler to claim five wickets in an innings in all three limited-overs competitions. His 5-26 in the Benson & Hedges was a county record whilst in the John Player League he was the first Notts bowler to take 100 wickets.

Brian Bolus described him as the 'greatest trier I've ever known', a player who always gave of his best and who always worked hard to improve his game. These qualities earned the respect of his fellow professionals, who on two occasions voted him the Cricketers' Cricketer.

Franklyn Dacosta Stephenson
RHB & RF, 1988-91

Born: 8 April, 1959, St James, Barbados

Batting

M	I	NO	Runs	HS
82	127	17	2845	121
89	69	18	1166	98*

Ave	50	100	ct/st
25.86	16	3	28
22.86	4	-	21

Bowling

Runs	Wkts	Av	BB	5wI	10wM
8124	349	23.28	8-47	23	6
2798	136	20.57	5-31	1	-

Best Performances
121 v. Leicestershire, Nottingham, 1990
98* v. Worcestershire, Nottingham, 1990
8-47 v. Essex, Nottingham, 1989
5-31 v. Northamptonshire, Wellingborough, 1991

The announcement that the West Indian all-rounder Franklyn Stephenson was to succeed Richard Hadlee as the county's overseas player for 1988 left Nottinghamshire supporters somewhat bemused and a little concerned, Stephenson having played in only nine first-class games in England for Gloucestershire in 1982 and 1983. A closer examination of his previous career revealed a match-winner that had achieved success both in the Lancashire League and for Tasmania and Barbados. A life ban after playing in a rebel tour of South Africa ended all hopes of playing any part in West Indian Test cricket.

As with Tasmania and Barbados, his debut season with Nottinghamshire in 1988 was an outstanding one, Stephenson being chosen as one of *Wisden*'s Five Cricketers of the Year and the Britannic Assurance Player of the Year. Consistently taking wickets throughout the season and claiming five wickets or more in an innings in seven of his last eight home appearances, he became the first to take a hundred wickets. In the final fixture of the season against Yorkshire at Trent Bridge, having scored 111 in the first innings, his first hundred since 1982, he still required 99 runs in the second to achieve the double. Coming in at 84-4, Stephenson went for his shots, hitting 20 fours and 2 sixes in his 117,

made in 137 minutes, thus becoming only the second player after Hadlee to complete the double since the reduction in Championship games. Earlier he had taken all the seven Yorkshire second innings wickets to fall before a declaration, his 11 wickets and his century making him the seventh Nottinghamshire player to score a century and take ten or more wickets in a match. His 2 centuries and ten or more wickets in a match made him only the third player in the history of the game to have achieved this feat, albeit the only one to finish on the losing side.

Stephenson continued to deliver match-winning performances for the next three seasons, heading the county's bowling averages in three in his four years and claiming the most wickets in each season. His career-best figures came in 1989 with match figures of 15-106 against Essex, the best achieved since Dooland in 1954. His 8-47 in the second innings against Essex was also a career-best performance. He appeared in every Championship game in 1991, also being the leading wicket-taker in the Sunday League, his thirty wickets assisting the county to win that competition for the first time. Four years after joining Nottinghamshire, he left to join Sussex, a move regretted by most supporters. Stephenson was a highly popular cricketer, not only because of his success on the field but because the Nottinghamshire public warmed to his affability and cheerfulness. In particular they will remember the antics of visiting batsmen, who failed miserably to deal with what became Stephenson's trademark, the beautifully concealed slower ball.

Born: 6 November 1918, Carcroft, Yorkshire
Died: 23 February 1996, Sutton-on-Sea, Lincolnshire

Batting

M	I	NO	Runs	HS
283	429	45	11378	171
Ave	50	100	ct/st	
29.63	65	13	155	

Bowling

Runs	Wkts	Av	BB	5wI	10wM
9794	223	43.91	6-37	6	-

Best Performances
171 v. Australians, Nottingham, 1956
6-37 v. Somerset, Nottingham, 1950

When Nottinghamshire began their first post-war Championship fixture against Kent at Trent Bridge, Freddie Stocks was the only player in the eleven not to have appeared in a first-class fixture. Before the end of the second day's play he had become the first Nottinghamshire batsman to score a century on his first-class debut, his 114 helping his side to win off the penultimate ball of the match. He remained the only county batsman to score a hundred on his Championship debut until Greg Blewett did so in 2002. Eight games later with his first ball in first-class cricket, he had Winston Place caught behind by Meads, thus completing a unique double. It proved to be an exciting first season for the twenty-seven year old, who played a part in the county's first three victories of the season. Against Worcestershire he made an unbeaten 100, featuring in an unbroken tenth-wicket partnership of 110 with Meads to help Notts gain an innings victory. In the following match against Hampshire at Portsmouth he remained unbeaten with wickets falling regularly as the county held on to win by one wicket, their closest wicket victory against another county since 1876. He was also chosen to take part in the Test Trial at Lord's for the Rest, the only occasion he was to appear in a first-class match for a team other than Nottinghamshire in his twelve-year career.

The son of a first-class cricketer, Stocks, Nottinghamshire-raised, played a number of games for Nottinghamshire during the war.

Stocks' career coincided with the county's worst set of results ever in the Championship, the county finishing in their lowest position – fifteenth in 1950 – only to suffer the indignity of last place in the following year. Stocks, who came into the side essentially as a middle-order left-hand batsman, found himself increasingly called upon to bowl, as the county searched desperately for support for Butler and Jepson. Beginning as a right-arm medium pacer, he proved extremely expensive but re-emerged as an off-spinner in 1950, achieving career-best figures of 6-37 in that year.

Stocks was equally accommodating with his batting, being prepared to bat in whichever position the team required and scoring quickly or defending stoutly as the situation demanded. Normally a number five batsman, he occasionally opened with Simpson, being involved in three century opening stands. His best season was 1951, when he scored 1,386 runs, 4 hundreds and bowled almost 600 overs. He reached 1,000 runs on five occasions between 1951 and 1956 when he was rarely out of the side and in his last full season, his benefit year, he played the highest innings of his career, 171 against the Australians, which is still a Nottinghamshire record. Stocks was a cheerful cricketer, whose determination and willingness to give his all for the county during some of its worst years earned him a deserved popularity amongst the county's followers.

Michael Norman Somerset Taylor
RHB & RM, 1964-72

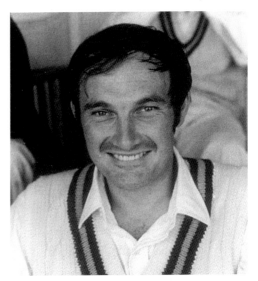

Born: 12 November 1942, Amersham, Buckinghamshire

Batting

M	I	NO	Runs	HS
230	320	77	4385	105
80	58	25	497	58

Ave	50	100	ct/st
18.04	13	1	139
15.06	1	-	28

Bowling

Runs	Wkts	Av	BB	5wI	10wM
14558	522	27.88	7-106	12	-
2718	107	25.40	4-20	-	-

Best Performances
105 v. Lancashire, Nottingham, 1967
58 v. Hampshire, Nottingham, 1972
7-106 v. Glamorgan, Nottingham, 1967
4-20 v. Surrey, Nottingham, 1969

Recruited from Buckinghamshire, Mike Taylor made his first-class debut for Nottinghamshire in 1964, becoming a permanent member of the First XI one year later. A right-arm medium-pace bowler and a useful lower-order batsman, he was an important ingredient in the side until he was surprisingly released by the county in 1972 after nine seasons, during which he hardly missed a game. In no sense a dominating player with either bat or ball, he fitted into that category of player who averaged around 500 runs and fifty wickets a season. Unfortunately in a county side which was constantly struggling to climb out of the bottom three of the Championship table, his efforts went largely unrewarded. He established himself in the side as a stock bowler in his first full season, initially providing support for Forbes and Corran. His first five wickets in an innings, 5-23 against Kent at Dover, included the hat-trick, his second victim being Colin Cowdrey. It was the first hat-trick by a Nottinghamshire bowler since Ken Smales achieved this feat in 1955. He also held six catches in the match against Surrey at The Oval, underlining his usefulness as a very reliable fielder close to the wicket, taking 26 catches in 1967, the most by a Nottinghamshire fielder in that year.

The year 1966 saw his most productive season with the bat, his 807 runs added to his 58 wickets, establishing his credentials as an all-rounder. This status was confirmed the following year when he took 83 wickets, including his best figures for the county, 7-106 against Glamorgan as well as recording his maiden century, 105 against Lancashire, his only one for the county. Thereafter his run output was to decline but he continued to take over fifty wickets a season for the remainder of his Notts career. His best season was undoubtedly 1968, when he failed by one single wicket to achieve 100 wickets in a season, topping the county's bowling averages with a highly economical average of 20.50.

During his final three seasons his wicket taking gradually became more expensive but his release in 1972 was still unexpected. In retrospect it appeared an error of judgement by the club. Taylor, taken on by Hampshire, was an ever-present and ended as a member of a Championship-winning side with 63 wickets to his credit. In comparison, Nottinghamshire finished in last place with no bowler taking fifty or more wickets. Taylor was to go on to play another seven seasons of first-class cricket, during which Hampshire won the John Player League on two occasions. A reminder of what his old county was missing came in his career-best figures of 7-23 against Notts in 1977 and an all-round performance of 5-29 and 68 in 1974, sending Notts to an innings defeat.

Robert Crispin Tinley

RHB & RF (round-arm), S (under-arm), 1847-69

Born: 25 October 1830, Southwell, Nottinghamshire
Died: 11 December 1900, Burton-on-Trent, Staffordshire

Batting

M	I	NO	Runs	HS
54	88	13	920	43
Ave	50	100	ct/st	
12.26	-	-	81	

Bowling

Runs	Wkts	Av	BB	5wI	10wM
1902	127+11	14.97	8-12	11	3

Best Performances
43 v. Kent, Cranbrook, 1863
8-12 v. Cambridgeshire, Nottingham, 1862

'Cris' Tinley was the youngest of three cricketing brothers to appear for Nottinghamshire. A local cricketer for Southwell Town Club, his success as a fast right-arm bowler in 1847 attracted the attention of the Nottinghamshire club, and Tinley made his debut in the county's only fixture against a unrepresentative England XI. At 16 years 288 days he still remains the youngest player to have appeared for the county.

Both his approach to batting and bowling changed during the mid-1850s. On his first appearance at Lord's in 1853 for Nottingham-shire against England, his batting was described as that of a slashing hard hitter, not especially stylish and not always hitting with a straight bat. He was also referred to as a very fast round-arm bowler. Richard Daft's description of Tinley in 1860 emphasises how Tinley's game had developed, stating he 'was far from being a slovenly slogger, for he hit invariably with a beautifully straight bat'. 'As an underhand bowler he was the best in England at that time.' Like other bowlers of his day he was attempting to emulate William Clarke's very successful bowling style, but he achieved far greater success than most. George Parr named him 'the Spider' and his combination with the 'Demon bowler' Jackson was described as one between the Thunderbolt and the Corkscrew.

His change of style certainly paid off for his county. His first thirteen appearances for the county bowling fast yielded twelve wickets, although in some games he was clearly selected for his batting, opening on a few occasions. Using his new style he took four wickets in an innings for the first time in 1858 and the following year he claimed 5-69 against Surrey at The Oval. By this time he had become an automatic selection for the county, missing only one of the county's thirty-six fixtures between 1858 and 1863. His great year for the county was 1862 when he claimed 30 wickets at a mere 8.76 apiece, turning in the best performance of his career, match figures of 15-78 against Cambridgeshire at Trent Bridge, including 8-12 in the first innings, still the least expensive 8-wicket analysis for the county. His last successful season for Nottinghamshire came three years later when he returned figures of 12-96 at Hove against Sussex. Incredibly he failed to take one wicket in his six appearances for Nottinghamshire in the following season and retired in 1867 after losing his place in the side.

He was in demand for many of the representative elevens of the day, the North, the Players and various England XIs. He remained an important member of Clarke's All England XI, appearing in an estimated 308 games in which he took 2,340 wickets.

William Voce
RHB & LFM/SLA, 1927-52

Born: 8 August 1909, Annesley Woodhouse, Nottinghamshire
Died: 6 June 1984, Nottingham

Batting

M	I	NO	Runs	HS
345	418	96	6398	129
Ave	50	100	ct/st	
19.86	24	4	243	

Bowling

Runs	Wkts	Av	BB	5wI	10wM
29207	1312	22.26	8-30	73	17

Best Performances

129 v. Glamorgan, Nottingham, 1931
8-30 v. Somerset, Weston-Super-Mare, 1939

Bill Voce will always be associated with Harold Larwood and the notorious 1932/33 Bodyline tour but like Larwood he was an immensely successful county cricketer, at his peak the best fast left-arm bowler of his day. Only Tom Wass has claimed more Championship wickets for the county and Voce is also one of the twelve Nottinghamshire players who have scored over 5,000 runs and taken over 500 wickets for the county. Less well known were his contributions in the field, both in the deep and at slip, in 1929 against Glamorgan becoming the first fielder to hold seven catches in a day's play. Initially a slow-medium spinner, he became, aged 17 years 321 days, the second youngest player to make his county debut in a Championship game. His 5-36 made him the seventh Notts bowler to achieve this feat on their Championship debut. From this point he was to retain an automatic place in the county side, barring injury and availability, until asked to be released in 1947. His early success prompted talk of him as a potentially great England spin bowler but although retaining and using this talent throughout his career, it was as a pace bowler that Voce was to make his name. Aided by both height and strength, with a beautifully easy action and a belligerent attitude, he was able to bowl fast with zip and bounce – a nasty proposition on a pitch giving help to pace and movement. Over the wicket he was capable of moving the ball both ways, this proving highly successful on his 1936/37 tour of

Australia. His round-the-wicket approach, coupled with the short-pitched ball, enabling him to slant the ball rib-high into the right-handed batsman, was eminently suited to the employment of fast-leg theory by both Carr and Jardine.

The 1929 season marked a significant advance in Voce's career. He played a key part in Nottinghamshire's Championship success, heading the county's bowling averages with 107 Championship wickets at 16.03 apiece. He recorded the county's fifth best-ever match figures, 14-43 against Northamptonshire, and was selected for the MCC touring party to the West Indies in 1929/30 at the age of twenty. Both this and his tour to South Africa the following winter enhanced his reputation, taking most wickets in both Test series. Considered a danger, the Australians successfully hit him out of contention for the 1930 Test series in their fixture against the county.

Voce's consistent good form as an opening bowler with Larwood, each taking over a hundred wickets in 1931 and 1932, earned him recognition as one of *Wisden*'s Five Cricketers of the Year in 1932. He achieved his best innings figures, 8-40 against Kent, and with Larwood bowled unchanged throughout the match against Leicestershire in 1932, Leicestershire's two innings lasting a mere 160 minutes. With both occasionally employing fast-leg theory for the county, they became essential ingredients in

Voce's partnership with Harold Larwood was one of the most feared in Championship cricket.

Injury and synovitis restricted his appearances in the remaining seasons before the war, although in 1939 he did achieve his best-ever innings analysis, 8-30 against Somerset. He was also beginning to revert to spin with considerable success in a number of matches. After the war he still showed glimpses of his old form, scoring an unbeaten 114*, which included 5 sixes and 11 fours, in 120 minutes against Derbyshire and taking 5-92 in the same match. His failure in Australia persuaded him to seek an early release from the county in 1947, although he appeared in a few games when required until 1952. He gave one last reminder of his capabilities in his penultimate appearance, taking 5-81 against Sussex, then going on to hit a rapid 45 in 30 minutes, hitting 3 sixes and 3 fours. It was reminder of his reputation as a hard-hitting and capable batsman, who scored 1,000 runs in 1933, achieved 4 first-class hundreds and struck 26 sixes in 1931. In that season he recorded the fastest century for the county, hitting 129 against Glamorgan in 75 minutes, reaching three figures in a mere 45 minutes, the fourth fastest century on record. In 1938 he struck 4 consecutive sixes off Mitchell of Derbyshire. He holds the record for participating in more tenth-wicket century partnerships, four in all, than any other Nottinghamshire player.

Jardine's strategy for the 1932/33 Bodyline series, although it proved to be one of Voce's less successful overseas tours. Passed over by the Selectors for the 1934 Tests against Australia despite taking 128 wickets at only 22 apiece, his annoyance at his omission surfaced in the county's game against the Australians. His short-pitched bowling earned him 8-66 in the first innings and two vitriolic overs in bad light on the second evening led to his absence on the third day suffering from 'sore shins', resulting in a major crisis in the county's affairs.

However, his excellent form from 1934 to 1936, when he claimed between 128 and 136 wickets each season, and his decision to make his peace with the Selectors earned him a place on the 1936/37 tour to Australia, where he headed the Test averages with 26 wickets at a mere 21.53 apiece, returning a match analysis of 10-57 in the First Test. In the Second he claimed three wickets in four balls in his first ten deliveries, including Bradman's first ball. It was to be the climax of his Test career, for he was to appear in only four more Tests; his last two appearances took place in Australia in 1946/47, when he was, at thirty-seven, both too old and too heavy to achieve anything of note. He was never selected against Australia in England.

After retiring from playing he retained his interest and his love of the game by becoming a coach at Trent Bridge and also at the MCC Indoor Cricket School at Lord's, where he was still bowling to schoolboys at the ripe old age of seventy. Len Hutton wrote that, 'He loved cricket just as much as he loved the Nottinghamshire mining community where he was born and bred and where he learnt his cricket.' It was an epitaph with which Bill Voce would have heartily agreed.

Willis Walker
RHB & RM, 1913-37

Born: 24 November 1892, Gosforth, Northumberland

Died: 3 December 1991, Keighley, Yorkshire

Batting

M	I	NO	Runs	HS
405	622	60	18242	165*
Ave	50	100	ct/st	
32.45	101	31	110	

Bowling

Runs	Wkts	Av	BB	5wI	10wM
97	2	48.50	2-20	-	-

Best Performances
165* v. Middlesex, Lord's, 1930
2-20 v. Worcestershire, Nottingham, 1926

A glance through the Nottinghamshire batting records does not reveal much about Willis Walker's significant contribution to the county's fortunes. He never reached 2,000 runs in a season, scored a double-century, carried his bat or scored two hundreds in a match. Yet he remains the seventeenth highest run-scorer for the county, thirteen of those above him having played for their country. He was, however, an integral part of the side in some of its most successful years, highly consistent and reliable; a truly dedicated professional. An orthodox batsman, he would today be termed a 'percentage player', or an accumulator, playing as Cardus remarked, 'by the book of arithmetic'. He was good to watch, described as an elegant strokemaker, immaculately turned out, and especially noted for his off-driving and leg-side placements. He remained extremely fit, also playing as a goalkeeper in the Football League for several clubs.

Although born in Northumberland he moved to Nottinghamshire as a child. He appeared in only a few games before the First World War, and then played in the Bradford League until he was invited to rejoin the county staff after a number of appearances in 1922. Although recording a maiden first-class hundred in 1923, he found it extremely difficult to break into the county's settled and experienced batting line-up, only becoming a permanent fixture at number three in the side in 1925. His contribution of over 1,300 runs and two centuries in that first full season became the norm for the next ten seasons. Only in 1934, when an attack of appendicitis limited his appearances, did he fail to reach 1,000 runs. He was never to average under thirty in any season from 1925 to 1935, on six occasions scoring over 1,500 runs and apart from 1934 always managing at least two hundreds. His most productive season came in 1933 when he scored 1,730 runs but his best year was the previous season when he scored five centuries and recorded an average in the mid-1940s. In all he scored 31 hundreds for the county but on only three occasions did he pass 150, a point underlined by his obituary in *Wisden*, which noted he was 'not hungry for runs'. Unflurried, he often held the side together in a crisis and was equally at ease as an opener, scoring two centuries in that position in 1926 when George Gunn was injured.

Walker played all but one of his first-class games for the county, his 405 appearances being the seventh highest for Nottinghamshire. His run of 124 consecutive games occurred between 1927 and 1931, at a time when Notts finished in the top five positions in the table, including being Championship winners in 1929. He began to lose his touch in 1936 and decided with no regrets to retire in 1937, remaining in the game as a coach at Charterhouse. On his death he was the oldest surviving first-class cricketer and the last survivor of pre-1914 Championship cricket. It was said that 'the limit of his ambition was to serve his county as well as he possibly could'. It was an ambition which was richly fulfilled.

Born: 26 December 1873, Sutton-in-Ashfield,
 Nottinghamshire
Died: 27 October 1953, Sutton-in-Ashfield,
 Nottinghamshire

Batting

M	I	NO	Runs	HS
308	388	97	2119	56
Ave	50	100	ct/st	
7.28	1	-	108	

Bowling

Runs	Wkts	Av	BB	5wI	10wM
33619	1653	20.33	9-67	158	44

Best Performances

56 v. Derbyshire, Chesterfield, 1906
9-67 v. Derbyshire, Blackwell, 1911

Apart from four other appearances – three times for the Players and once for an England XI – Tom Wass played all his cricket for his native county. A miner from Sutton-in-Ashfield, the great nursery of Nottinghamshire cricketers, his talents as a fast bowler were soon recognised, Wass taking up professional engagements from the age of twenty. Lancashire County Cricket were sufficiently interested to offer him a position on the county's ground staff, but Wass declined the offer, subsequently being invited to join the Nottinghamshire club, after dismissing Arthur Shrewsbury on a number of occasions in the nets, something which allegedly had not been done for years.

Although making his first-class debut in 1896 other professional engagements prevented him establishing a permanent place in the side until 1898. A late starter in the first-class game, not making his mark until the age of twenty-five, he went on to become the highest wicket-taker in the county's history, his final tally of 1,653 wickets eclipsing all other figures. The capture of five wickets in an innings on 158 occasions in 308 fixtures is another staggering statistic, equivalent to approximately once every second game.

Wass was played solely as a bowler for he was both a poor batsman and a very indifferent fielder, usually stationed at mid-on. A tall, six-footer, powerfully built, with a high side-on action, he possessed the strength to bowl tirelessly for long spells if necessary. His main strength as a fast bowler came from his ability to bowl a fast leg-break or leg-cutter, which at time came back from outside leg-stump to take the off-stump or provoked a snick to the waiting slips or gully. How he achieved this fast leg-break, whether deliberately or simply the natural consequence of his action is debatable but it made Wass a highly individualistic bowler, capable of bowling a virtually unplayable ball at times. He was particularly difficult to play on soft pitches, affected by rain, *Wisden* commenting in 1906 that 'on his day and his own wicket, he was one of the most difficult bowlers now before the public.'

Wass first claimed a hundred wickets in a season in 1900, forming a highly successful opening attack with John Gunn. An indifferent season followed, Wass being dropped for the only time in his career but he bounced back in his comeback game against Derbyshire with his best innings figures to date, 8-17. He struck up a highly successful partnership with Hallam, the pair bowling unchanged in a match on four occasions, and after Hallam's retirement Wass achieved this once more with Iremonger in 1913. From 1900 Wass bore the brunt of the

Wass (second from right) was one of the greatest bowlers never to have been selected for his country.

Nottinghamshire attack, seven times finishing at the head of the county's averages and being the leading wicket-taker on five other occasions. His reputation of being virtually unplayable when the pitch suited him is borne out by a number of devastating bowling spells, when he literally ran through the opposing batting. Twice he was to take sixteen wickets in a day, first against Lancashire in 1906 at Liverpool and again in 1908 against Essex at Trent Bridge, taking eight wickets in each innings, and having a deadly spell of six wickets for nine runs in eighteen balls in the first. The best innings return of his career, 9-67 against Derbyshire in 1911, the second time he had taken nine wickets in an innings, included a spell of 8 for 19.

His greatest season came in 1907 when he and Hallam bowled Nottinghamshire to the Championship. In a wet summer with pitches suiting Wass to perfection, his contribution was 145 Championship wickets at 13.07 apiece. In all games he claimed 163 wickets, easily beating his own county record of 140 set in 1902. In nineteen Championship matches he claimed wickets in every game bar one, a match against Yorkshire restricted through rain to 45 minutes. On two occasions with Hallam he bowled unchanged throughout the match and Wass himself was unchanged in eight other innings. In all Wass and Hallam took 319 of the 379 wickets captured by the county bowlers in that year, a remarkable tour de force. Both were named as *Wisden*'s Cricketers of the Year in recognition of their achievements.

He was to take over a hundred wickets a season on ten occasions, missing this target by only two wickets in 1913, his penultimate first-class season as a regular member of the side. This total remains a county record, as is his achievement of taking over fifty wickets in sixteen individual seasons. Such performances inevitably raise the question posed in his obituary in *Wisden* that 'it was remarkable that in view of his many successes, he was never chosen for England.' It was also a question asked of Tom Oates, the county scorer by John Arlott, Oates replying that 'Tom

were a roogh diamond.' Arlott persisted, arguing that this hadn't prevented others playing for England, to which Oates replied, 'Ay, but Tom were roogher'n most.'

Wass, known as 'Topsy' to his friends, certainly earned a reputation for outspokenness and his clashes with amateurs of the day made the rounds of the county dressing rooms. In particular he found C.B. Fry, known as 'Cocky' by the Nottinghamshire professionals, especially irksome. Once addressed simply as Wass by Fry, Tom had retorted, 'It's Mister Wass to buggers such as thee.' On another occasion, when Fry stepped back from the crease as Wass was running into bowl on the grounds, that there was movement behind the bowler, Wass remarked, 'Look here, Mr Fry, the next time you come to Nottingham, we'll have pavilion shifted for you.' Such comments did not endear himself to cricket's establishment. However, his poor standard of batting and fielding may also have counted against him, as well as a reputation, somewhat unfounded, of being a bad wicket bowler, who found it more difficult to take wickets on good pitches. Whatever the reasons, he remains as one of the greatest bowlers the county has ever produced and would figure highly in any team of the best players never to have been chosen for England.

Brian Douglas Wells

RHB & OB, 1960-65

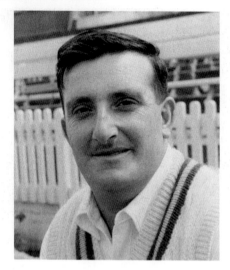

Born: 27 July 1930, Gloucester

Batting

M	I	NO	Runs	HS
151	217	59	1281	55
3	2	0	5	5
Ave	50	100	ct/st	
8.10	1	-	46	
2.50	-	-	-	

Bowling

Runs	Wkts	Av	BB	5wI	10wM
12052	429	28.09	7-34	17	2
101	2	50.50	1-31	-	-

Best Performances

55 v. Glamorgan at Swansea, 1962
5 v. Somerset, Taunton, 1964
7-34 v. Worcestershire, Nottingham, 1963
1-31 v. Yorkshire, Middlesbrough, 1963

Although 'Bomber' Wells has always remained a Gloucestershire man through and through, it comes as something of a surprise to discover that he was to feature in more games for Nottinghamshire than his own home county. His fine off-spin bowling, which had yielded 544 wickets at a mere 21.18 apiece, came at a time when Gloucestershire was awash with equally talented bowlers. Unathletic, comparatively slow in the field and a 'six or nought' batsman, he simply could not compete with his main rivals, John Mortimore and David Allen.

Nottinghamshire, with a woefully thin attack after the departure of Dooland, were only too willing to sign Wells by special registration. If there was to be little improvement in the county's standing in the six seasons he stayed with the club, little of the fault could be laid at his door. He might have joked that he 'filled the gap between Bruce Dooland and Gary Sobers' but along with Bruce Dooland and Ken Smales he is the only spinner to take over a hundred wickets in a season for Notts since the war. His first season, in which he appeared in all thirty games, brought him 120 wickets at 24.25 apiece, beginning with 5-74 on his debut against Cambridge University. He took wickets in all four of the county's victories that season, his best performance being against Glamorgan when his match figures of 11-97, included 5-11 as Glamorgan were bowled out for 52. In that year he bowled 1354.3 overs, the most by any bowler in the country, although his maximum two-step run-up

was a key element in this total. Wells was denied a hundred wickets in two other seasons by unusual circumstances. Requiring seven wickets from the last innings of the county's last fixture of 1961 against Hampshire, he took the first six wickets to fall, only for a declaration to leave him one short. Two years later rain limited Wells to just eight overs in the last match of the season, leaving him four short of the hundred. Not that Bomber was one for statistics or records, even when he fell short of 1,000 wickets in his career by two.

He bowled over 1,000 overs in each of his first four seasons and was never to miss a Championship match. When he was eventually left out of the side midway through 1964 he had appeared in 123 consecutive Championship fixtures and missed only two other non-Championship games. He topped the county's bowling averages in his first two years and also enjoyed the only fifty of his career in 423 innings, his 55 against Glamorgan being a typical Wells innings, struck in 30 minutes and including 5 sixes and 4 fours.

One of the game's great post-war characters and the centre of innumerable stories and anecdotes, often related by himself, Wells provided a cheery interlude both on and off the field at a time when the county's fortunes were at their lowest ebb.

Robert Arthur White
LHB & OB, 1966-80

Born: 6 October 1936, Fulham, London

Batting

M	I	NO	Runs	HS
298	448	80	8259	116*
165	115	38	1351	86*
Ave	50	100	ct/st	
22.44	32	3	142	
17.54	2	-	44	

Bowling

Runs	Wkts	Av	BB	5wI	10wM
21102	693	30.45	7-41	28	4
3736	136	27.47	4-15	-	-

Best Performances
116* v. Surrey, The Oval, 1967
86 v. Surrey, Guildford, 1973*
7-41 v. Derbyshire, Ilkeston, 1971
4-15 v. Somerset, Bath, 1975

Bob White's first-class career stretched over four decades, with eight seasons with Middlesex and the remaining fifteen with Nottinghamshire. For many years he was indispensable to the Nottinghamshire side, especially in the 1970s, missing only three Championship matches out of a total of 170 between 1970 and 1977, being ever present in four seasons and appearing in 100 consecutive games.

Taken on initially as a useful and versatile left-hand middle-order batsman, with some experience as an opener, he was to fill both roles for the county, although he was never to capture his 1963 batting form, being essentially a 500 to 700 runs-a-year man, with an average hovering in the mid-twenties. His best individual performance came early in his Notts career, when he struck a career-best 116* against Surrey at The Oval, sharing at the time a record 204 for the seventh wicket with Mike Smedley. Two more centuries followed, perhaps his most satisfying being an unbeaten 114 whilst opening against Middlesex at Lord's in 1972, his 788 Championship runs in that year being his highest for the county.

His great value to the Nottinghamshire side was his totally unexpected contribution as an off-spinner, having bowled a mere 33 overs during his 114 matches for Middlesex. Introduced into the attack, White played an important part in the first success of 1966 with 5-35 against Hampshire. He gradually became the premier slow bowler in the side, a position he was to occupy with little competition until the advent of Hemmings. He was essentially steady, depending on line and length rather than spin and putting in his 500 plus overs each season. His best year was 1971 when he topped the county's bowling averages, taking 81 wickets in all matches. His career-best bowling figures came against Derbyshire in that same season, when only the weather prevented him from returning his best ever match figures. Taking a career-best 7 wickets for 41 runs in the first innings, he took the first three in the second innings before rain ended the match, leaving White with 10 of the 13 wickets to have fallen at a cost of 51 runs. He continued to pick up fifty or more wickets in a season until 1978 when the reshaping of the county side restricted his appearances. He captained the Second XI in 1979, but returned, aged forty-three, in his penultimate first-class game, taking 10-57, the third occasion he had claimed ten wickets in a match. His 6-24 in the second innings helped to dismiss Derbyshire for 54, giving Notts a surprise victory. He became assistant manager in 1982 before joining the first-class umpire's list until retiring in 2001. Described in a *Wisden* article as one of the 'willing workhorses of first-class cricket', it was a description with which Bob White would probably concur.

Born: 31 October 1887, Woodborough, Nottinghamshire
Died: 11 November 1930, Nottingham

Batting

M	I	NO	Runs	HS
346	560	42	20376	248
Ave	50	100	ct/st	
39.33	95	50	286/14	

Bowling

Runs	Wkts	Av	BB	5wI	10wM
191	6	31.83	3-49	-	-

Best Performances

248 v. Northamptonshire, Nottingham, 1930
3-49 v. Middlesex, Lord's, 1921

The most striking feature of 'Dodge' Whysall's career was a prodigious output of runs in his final five seasons, when, over thirty-eight years of age, he recorded an aggregate of over 2,000 runs per season. It was all the more tragic that two months after the close of the 1930 season, he should suffer a minor fall and die of septicaemia a few weeks later. It was the culmination of a career which began with his first-class debut in 1910 against Derbyshire. Not only did he reach fifty in his first-ever first-class innings, he enjoyed a century opening partnership with George Gunn, a forerunner of one of the most successful opening partnerships in the county's history. They provided a formidable opening partnership in the 1920s, opening on 405 occasions and being involved in 40 century partnerships, averaging just over forty and four times passing 200. Whysall made a slow start in the first-class game, his maiden century coming in 1914 against the MCC at Lord's, but he found it difficult to break into a settled batting line-up until 1922. His first year of real success came in 1924, his 1,786 runs in the Championship being the most in that competition. A purple patch in June brought him 4 hundreds in consecutive games, 2 double-century opening partnerships with George Gunn and 1,000 runs for the season, the first batsman to reach this target. He was named one of *Wisden's* Five Cricketers of the Year and selected for the winter tour of Australia.

From 1924 to 1930, Whysall headed the county's batting averages on five occasions and established a number of new county records. His last five seasons brought him 33 centuries, including 3 double-centuries, twice scoring two hundreds in a match, out of his final total of 50 hundreds for the county. His aggregate of 9 hundreds in 1928 was a county record as was his total aggregate of 2,716 runs in 1929, the highest by a Nottinghamshire batsman in one season. His tally of 2,458 in Championship matches alone the previous season was again a record for the county. During his final season in 1930 he became the only Nottinghamshire batsman to score four consecutive hundreds, part of a sequence of seven innings of over fifty.

Whysall was to appear in only four Tests, three on the Australian tour of 1924/25 and one at The Oval in 1930, on the former tour acting as reserve wicketkeeper. Not a stylish batsman, he adopted an almost full-face stance to the bowler, he did possess infinite patience and an ability to play within his limitations. In *Wisden* it was once suggested that he never looked as good as he was. His career figures are proof enough that he ranks as one of the most successful batsmen ever to play for the county. His county captain Arthur Carr certainly thought so. He awarded talent money to his professionals, giving them a mark, worth five shillings, for any outstanding performance. Whysall was the player who earned the most talent money in any one season, no less than £40 in 1929, the year Nottinghamshire won the County Championship.

Francis Gerald Woodhead
RHB & RFM, 1934-50

Born: 30 October 1912, Edwinstowe, Nottinghamshire
Died: 24 May 1991, Nottingham

Batting

M	I	NO	Runs	HS
141	174	44	1100	52*
Ave	50	100	ct/st	
8.46	1	-	80	

Bowling

Runs	Wkts	Av	BB	5wI	10wM
10550	320	32.96	7-24	11	1

Best Performances
52* v. Hampshire, Nottingham, 1936
7-24 v. Worcestershire, Nottingham, 1938

Frank Woodhead joined the county in 1934 as a fast-medium bowler, creating a favourable impression with his performances in the Second XI. It was a time when the county's previously strong bowling attack strength was in a state of flux, with Larwood, Sam Staples and Arthur Staples all retiring in the late 1930s. Woodhead initially filled in on a number of occasions for Larwood but took full advantage of his limited chances the following season, heading the Championship averages with 22 wickets at only 20.63 apiece. Towards the end of the season he also recorded five wickets in an innings for the first time, claiming 6-28 against Warwickshire. For the remaining four seasons prior to the war, he was one of three young bowlers competing for a place in the side, but was never able to cement a permanent place. With Butler missing a large part of the 1938 season, Woodhead became one of the regular opening bowlers, responding with 69 wickets at 25.04, enough to again place him at the head of the county's averages. He ended the season with both career-best innings and match figures, 7-24 and 10-94 respectively, against Worcestershire.

Building upon his success in 1938, he began 1939 with appearances in the first five games but was mysteriously left out of the side after taking 5-51 against Leicestershire, Jepson being preferred as first change, Woodhead only returning in the penultimate game to take 5-97. He

returned 7-41 in his second post-war game, taking a creditable 58 wickets in the 1946 season on the inhospitable Trent Bridge pitch, again taking over fifty wickets for the third and last time in 1949. This was his last full season when, with Butler injured, he opened the bowling; bowling more overs, 829, than ever before. However, the performance which remains in the memory of those who supported the county in the immediate post-war years came in 1948, when he clean bowled Bradman, Hassett and Miller in the Australians' first innings against the county.

A negligible batsman, he passed fifty only once, an unbeaten 52* in 1936, part of a tenth-wicket partnership of 75 with Harold Butler. On retirement a successful spell as coach at the Nottingham High School led him back to the county, first as captain of the newly-formed Notts Colts in the mid-1960s, then as county coach between 1970 and 1980 and also as liaison officer with schools and youth cricket. His pride in being associated with the Nottinghamshire club was reflected in his creation of the Old Players Association in 1961, for which he remained secretary for twenty years. Having played his entire first-class cricket in a Nottinghamshire side composed entirely of Nottinghamshire men, he was determined to reverse the trend in the late 1960s when the county side was almost bereft of local players. His work bore fruit as players of the calibre of Cooper, French, Randall and Birch began to force their way into the county XI. He fully deserved a testimonial in 1979, celebrating his commitment to the county over so many years.

Born: 16 October 1834, Clifton, Nottinghamshire
Died: 15 June 1924, Ruddington, Nottinghamshire

Batting

M	I	NO	Runs	HS
52	82	16	701	60*
Ave	50	100	ct/st	
10.62	2	-	35	

Bowling

Runs	Wkts	Av	BB	5wI	10wM
2832	181	15.64	7-33	11	1

Best Performances
60* v. Kent, Nottingham, 1869
7-33 v. Cambridgeshire, Cambridge, 1862

Although George Wootton made a belated entrance into top-class cricket, supposedly because of his shy, retiring nature, his subsequent career has been described in *Scores and Biographies* as 'brief and brilliant'. Appearing against the MCC at Lord's for a Colts XI, his match figures of 8-75 accelerated him into the Nottinghamshire XI, for whom he appeared in 52 out of a possible 57 games, his absences mostly caused by injury or other playing commitments. He joined a formidable Nottinghamshire bowling attack in 1861, comprising Jackson, Tinley and Grundy, later to be joined by J.C. Shaw and Alfred Shaw. Standing at only 5ft 6in, Wootton's medium-pace left-arm bowling involved a low delivery, producing a considerable number of 'shooters', which was to yield him many of his greatest bowling triumphs.

He began well, taking 5-25 in his second appearance for the county against Surrey at Trent Bridge in 1861, and achieved his best-ever innings figures for Nottinghamshire in the first game of the following season, 7-33 against Cambridgeshire. He was to take five or more wickets in an innings on a further nine occasions for the county but only managed to secure ten wickets in a match once, 10-96 against Lancashire at Trent Bridge in 1868. This was his best season for the county, taking 27 wickets in six appearances at a cost of 11.51 apiece. On seven occasions he bowled unchanged with his opening partner, usually Grundy or J.C. Shaw,

dismissing Sussex for 38 with Grundy at Trent Bridge in 1865, and Kent for 52 and 43 with J.C. Shaw in 1869 and 1870. Against Yorkshire in 1866 at Trent Bridge he bowled unchanged throughout the match as the visitors were bowled out for 78 and 83. A left-handed batsman, he began his career with four consecutive noughts but developed as a free-hitting lower order batsman. In making his highest score for Nottinghamshire, an unbeaten 60*, he assisted W. McIntyre in putting on 165 for the ninth wicket against Kent at Trent Bridge in 1869, which remained a record for this wicket until 1994.

Twice he took nine wickets in an innings at Lord's, also claiming a hat-trick during an analysis of 8-9. The best innings figures of his career were 10-54 against Yorkshire at Sheffield. Wootton took 100 wickets in a season in four consecutive seasons between 1866 and 1869, being the only bowler to achieve this feat in 1866. In 1867 and 1869 he was the first to reach this target. His best year was 1867, when he claimed 142 wickets at 11.57 apiece.

Wootton retired in 1871 against the wishes of the Nottinghamshire club, stating that 'he thought cricket had left him'. He became a first-class umpire until 1881 and retained his interest in cricket almost to the end of his life, attending the 1921 Test Match at Trent Bridge at the age of eighty-six. He died three years later, at eighty-nine years of age, being one of the county's longest survivors.

Born: 27 May 1863, Harewood, Yorkshire
Died: 10 January 1936, Saxelby Park, Melton Mowbray, Leicestershire

Batting

M	I	NO	Runs	Av
117	197	5	2565	99
Ave	50	100	ct/st	
13.35	14	-	60/6	

Best Performances
99 v. Sussex, Hove, 1882

Of all the Nottinghamshire players who have appeared for England, Charles Wright is arguably the least well known. He toured on four occasions with Lord Hawke's teams (Hawke had been Wright's captain at Cambridge), the visit in 1895/96 to South Africa earning him three Test appearances. He thus became the first Nottinghamshire cricketer to play against South Africa, although these England XIs were in no way representative of England's cricketing strength.

Although his career proved a modest one, he was seen as a highly promising young player, acclaimed as the best public school wicketkeeper in 1881, winning four Blues at Cambridge University and in 1883 scoring 102 in the Varsity match. He also appeared for the Gentlemen, but achieved little in his nine appearances. His success at this stage had been assisted by the coaching he had received from the professional coaches at Trent Bridge, his father William Wright being an influential individual in cricketing circles in Yorkshire and Nottinghamshire.

Wright made his debut in 1882 whilst still at university, scoring 99 in his first season against Sussex at Hove, his highest innings for the county. It was typical of many innings he was to play as an opening bat, being last out, having batted for 270 minutes. He often proved difficult to dislodge, batting for an hour for one run against Middlesex in 1894. His strong defence enabled him to carry his bat for 7* out of 51 for Staffordshire's XI against the Australians, having scored 26 out of 60 in the first innings. Against MCC at Lord's in 1891 he opened the innings, being last out, having scored 5 in the

Notts total of 21 and in the second innings making 39 out of 69, the game being completed in one day.

He made only irregular appearances in the 1880s, missing the whole of 1886 after sustaining a severe head injury when kicked by a horse. With the county beginning to lose the great players of the previous decade, he appeared more regularly in the 1890s and as an amateur was called upon to captain the side on twenty-six occasions, with little success, the county only claiming four victories under his leadership. He became the first Notts captain to declare an innings closed, this being against Kent in 1890 and was also responsible for the county dispensing with the services of one of its best bowlers, Frank Shacklock, after reporting him to the committee for drinking. He kept wicket in 1895 but proved not to be up to standard.

He became the fourth batsman to be given out handled ball, clearly a Notts tradition, as two of the previous three were also Nottinghamshire players. After removing the ball from his pads on appeal from W.G. Grace and asked why he had removed the ball, Wright replied 'I didn't want it there!' His association with the county continued after the end of his playing career, hastened by the loss of an eye in a shooting incident; he became a trustee and also treasurer till his death in 1936.

Frederick Wyld
RHB & RF (round-arm) & WK, 1868-81

Born: 28 August 1847, Eastwood, Nottinghamshire
Died: 11 February 1893, Nottingham

Batting

M	I	NO	Runs	HS
109	177	13	2726	104
Ave	50	100	ct/st	
16.62	7	1	107/25	

Bowling

Runs	Wkts	Av	BB	5wI	10wM
93	7	13.28	4-33	-	-

Best Performances
104 v. Gloucestershire, Nottingham, 1872
4-33 v. Gloucestershire, Nottingham, 1871

Frederick Wyld's major claim to fame in the county's history was his achievement of recording the first century by a Nottinghamshire batsman at Trent Bridge, reaching this milestone against Gloucestershire in 1872. Just as important, however, was his willingness to put his county's needs before his own, for many years filling in as stop-gap wicketkeeper, something which was to have eventually a detrimental effect on his batting.

Wyld was a collier who played initially for a great local patron of the game, Squire Walker of Eastwood Hall. Wyld in 1868 scored a half-century against the All England XI and was selected for the XXII Colts against Nottinghamshire, doing enough with the bat to gain selection for the county side against Surrey at The Oval. He became a regular member of the county side, rarely missing a game except through injury until his penultimate season in 1880. Wyld was an aggressive batsman, who played shots all round the wicket, with a reputation for big hitting. He soon confirmed his early promise, averaging almost thirty in his first full season for the club in 1868. He had an outstanding season for Nottinghamshire in 1872, averaging 32.10 and scoring his noteworthy 104 at Trent Bridge. He headed the county's batting averages for the first and only time in 1875, just missing a second hundred for the

club, when he scored 93 against Derbyshire at Derby.

The year 1876 proved to be something of a turning point in Wyld's career, for he was called upon to keep wicket after the sad early death of Sam Biddulph. Although the county possessed a specialist 'keeper in Mordecai Sherwin, who was clearly far superior to Wyld, the committee decided to keep with Wyld on account of his better batting for the foreseeable future. The subsequent damage to Wyld's hands resulted in a rapid decline in his batting and a gradual drop down the order.

By 1879 his batting average had fallen to 8.79 and after he had reached a top-score of only four in his first six innings of 1880 Sherwin replaced him. This would probably have been his last season for the county but the strike by seven of the leading professionals in 1881 led to his recall purely as a batsman for a further eight games in that year. His average of 20.90, his best for seven seasons, illustrates how much his batting had suffered as a consequence of his 'keeping. His prowess as a batsman was recognised in his three appearances for the Players, his engagement with the MCC from 1875 until 1887, and his many appearances for the All England XI. He made one other first-class hundred, an unbeaten 104* for MCC against Cambridge University in 1877 at Lord's, which was described as another fine hitting display.